WWW.EMPOWERME.ORG

Also By Adrienne Graham

Go Ahead, Talk to Strangers: The Modern Girl's Guide to Fearless Networking

Fearless Networking Without Asking Permission

Get Recruited: Secrets from a Top Recruiter on Using Unconventional Tactics to Get Noticed in an Inconvenient Economy

No, You *Can't* Pick My Brain

It Costs Too Much

⌘

Adrienne Graham

EMPOWER ME! PUBLISHING

WWW.EMPOWERME.ORG

Copyright ©2012 by Adrienne Graham. All Rights Reserved.

ISBN Number: 978-0-9824231-6-5

ISBN Number: 978-0-9824231-8-9 (e-book)

No part of this book may be reproduced or transmitted in any form or by any means, electronic or mechanical for any purpose without express written permission of Adrienne Graham.

For information about permission to reproduce selections from this book, contact the author at:

Empower Me! Corporation
P.O. Box 863, Alpharetta, GA 30009-0863 USA
+1 (866) 810-2525
www.empowerme.org

Published by Empower Me! Publishing dba Empower Me! Corporation.

Printed in the United States of America.

This book is dedicated to all of the hardworking professionals and business owners who work hard to service their clients and still manage to do good deeds.

It is also dedicated to my son Jason Seaton, Matthew Boyd, Mom & Dad, and the rest of my family for being understanding and supportive. I love you all.

To the many people who made my Forbes article such a hot topic, Thank You for chiming in and sharing your experiences. I hope this book serves you well.

And to the habitual brain pickers....kick rocks!

Table of Contents

Introduction

*Z*ig Ziglar perfected a saying: *"If you help enough people get what they want, you'll eventually get what you want"*. As crazy as it sounds, given the title of this book, I actually agree with this saying. I have benefited from and paid this mantra forward to many people. I have spent most of my professional life giving to people…many people, and I don't regret a minute of it. As I was growing in my career and my business, I found myself on my own a lot. But when I started to mature and learned to network and align myself with like-minded people, I noticed more people were willing to help me with no strings attached. I guess you can say that's when truly I learned to help others with no strings attached.

I'm a firm believer in helping people. But I equally believe that there should be a line drawn in the sand that applies to everyone no matter how new or experienced you are in your line of business. Otherwise your help can turn into enablement or kindness could be abused. We should *teach a man to fish instead of giving him the fish*. So we have to get comfortable learning to firmly tell some people NO.

I got the inspiration for this book after writing a blog post in March 2011, watching it go viral like wildfire on Forbes.com and reading the reactions of the many people who felt liberated by reading my words. It was bananas. Well what's even more bananas is I would occasionally work on the book, then I'd get sidetracked with life and other things. People would occasionally mention the post and send me kudos in email or via Twitter. But for the most part, it was just there on Forbes for anyone to see.

Then something wonderfully strange happened. I woke up on the morning of January 3, 2012 only to find that the article had once again gone viral. WOW! I couldn't believe it. So I had to rewrite the Introduction and finally complete this book.

When I went to bed on January 2, 2012, I had a plan and focus already laid out. But when I woke up the morning of January 3rd, it seemed God (and my readers) had other plans! People were emailing and tweeting me congratulating and thanking me for my *Forbes article*. I was a bit confused because Forbes and I had severed our relationship back in November, and I hadn't written anything for them since maybe August. They claimed they were "*going in a different direction editorially*" so my writing style no longer fit them. By the way, I was invited to write for Harvard Business Review, so look out for my work there! I know, shameless plug.

So I started investigating what all the commotion was about and I was floored to see that *No, You Can't Pick My Brain* had been resurrected. That's when I knew that I had to come back and put the finishing touches on this book, and I got a few new inspirations to add to it. Let me give you a little background about this book.

The blog post idea came from a social media buddy posting a simple question on her Facebook page one Saturday morning in March 2011. She asked if we ever got tired of giving away information for free to people who expected to get freebies all the time (or something to that effect). As I was responding, I felt this surge rise up in me. Not an angry surge, but a surge nonetheless. It made me stop and think. I freely give so much, but I've conditioned people to take it on faith that everything I do should be for free. Was I resentful? Maybe a little bit. Like I said, I don't mind helping others. But it did get me thinking about how I need to conduct myself, and have people view me moving forward as a businesswoman and a professional. In order to be

4

taken serious, I had to have a clearly drawn line in the sand.

That blog post struck a nerve (and continues to) in a lot of people. Many agreed, some disagreed, but the conversation was started and that's all that mattered. I wasn't the first person to express these opinions and I won't be the last. I had no idea how many people would be touched by this rant I posted. Scores of people shared their experiences and expressed their frustrations, but many said I gave them confirmation that they weren't wrong for feeling as they did. They felt like finally someone had given them permission to be OK with not wanting to continue to have their brains picked and dissected for free.

I was both amused and surprised at some of the stories that were shared. The comments didn't just stop at my own article. People passed and shared this article all over the web, and wrote their own reviews and variations of my article on their blogs and websites. In fact as I write this book, I am still getting requests from people for permission to reprint/repost the article. The stories ranged from the frustrated home-based business mom who constantly gets roped into *favors* and *freebies* because after all, she works from home (who can take her serious as a professional); to the business consultant who constantly gets used for his knowledge by people too cheap to pay for his advice. The stories varied but the sentiment was the same. People, especially those in the service industry, are tired of being used and not *valued* for their expertise. They have spoken and their knowledge deserves a premium.

At what point do we as professionals place a premium on ourselves and make others honor that premium? Where do we draw the line at *well-meaning free advice* and *billable hours*? When do we learn to tell people *no, you can't pick my brain*? As

I was reading the comments to my article, I realized there are a lot of people out there who are confused by the etiquette of "free". They don't know how or when to tell people no and charge for *consulting services* cleverly disguised as *advice*. They're afraid that if they start saying no, somehow they will inherit bad karma or that people won't want to help them any more. That is simply not true!

I love giving advice. I write blogs, articles and a newsletter. I host a weekly radio show dispensing advice. And if you follow me on social media, you'd know how much I tweet, Facebook and share nuggets of advice almost daily. Each year I choose to gift my services to deserving individuals who otherwise wouldn't be able to afford my services. The only real requirement I have is they pay it forward to others.

So what is it in all of that giving that makes anyone think they still have the right to continue *picking my brain* for free? When is enough, enough? Just because I choose to share some information and knowledge in public forums doesn't mean all of my advice or time is free. Now before you label me cheap, selfish or self-centered or my favorite "pissy" (I was called that by a commenter who read the article, and I still laugh), let's look at this logically. My knowledge and time used for implementation of said knowledge is how I make my living. Am I supposed to let my house get foreclosed on, go without food, or have my utilities shut off simply because people think I shouldn't charge for my knowledge? Would you work at your job for no paycheck? My knowledge is my business, my business is my job, and my *job* pays my bills. So I don't feel guilty at all. And neither should you.

I can't tell you how flattering it is to be approached by

representatives from major companies seeking my wisdom and advice. It shows they are listening, they like what I have to say and view me as a thought leader or subject matter expert. But often I find that bubble bursts when I discover they are just on a fact-finding mission. That mission is to pick my brain to gather as much free intel and knowledge as they need to make *their* jobs easier or impress their boss. Not gonna happen, sorry.

My brain costs money to maintain. There are ongoing training, classes to attend, reading (I do have to buy books), gaining certifications, costs of memberships so I can network, attending conferences and mastering my skills. That all costs me money and time. I have to protect my investment. How fair is it to me to give away all the knowledge I have acquired that I use to make my living, pay my bills and eat just to make someone else's life easier?

Now, don't get offended. If you do get offended, maybe you deserve to be because you're one of those brain pickers. I found that the only ones who took offense to my blog post and my stance on brain-picking are the very ones who like to pick, pick, pick at other people's brains. They like to absorb as much information for free as they can, all the while avoiding ever coming out of pocket. They may be the cheap stingy type, or maybe the victim of an employer with a budget. By far my favorite are the friends and family members who feel because they know me, grew up with me, or are in some way related to me, I should be giving out freebies and happy to do it! HAH! I don't think so. Well whoever they are, the brain-picking has to end.

You've probably purchased this book because you've been a victim of brain-picking (I do mention that term a LOT in this book, so get used to it). Just do a Google search of *"No, You Can't Pick My Brain"* and you'll likely see that you are not alone. Many people suffer from this and have no idea how to handle it. So don't feel like you're alone. You are not a terrible person for feeling this way and you deserve to have your knowledge and skills respected. There have been many articles written and discussions about this subject. It will be around for a long time.

With the Internet being so widely available and loaded with free information, people automatically assume that you too have to provide them information for free. My response to that is go ahead and read the free stuff. But when you still find yourself lacking answers, that apparently means the FREE stuff doesn't always work. You can't come to a professional and ask them to work for *free*. In essence, that is what you're doing when you ask to pick someone's brain. But yet, that's what some people do. And they do it without any thought or hesitation because they want what they want.

Let's put it in perspective for a moment. How would you feel if your boss came to you and said *"hey since we can get this done from information from the Internet, I won't be paying you today. After all, all we had to do was look it up the things you do on the Internet and we got it for free. So we really don't need to waste money on paying you"*.

Go ahead, let it sink in for a moment. Got that visual yet? Do you feel violated, used, taken advantage of? Good. That's exactly how I feel whenever someone wants to take me to lunch or call me to pick my brain. It feels like a violation and disrespect of my skills. *Oh Adrienne knows what to do. She'll just tell me.*

If you're like how I used to be, you've given away tons of

valuable information. I've never once minded helping people out who legitimately needed my help. I believe we all have a responsibility to give back. But it's the ones who keep coming back for more freebies and those who take my ideas, implement them, find success, then never offer to repay me for my time that irk me to no end. How selfish and self-serving can one be? And no, a turkey sandwich does NOT constitute adequate payment for me helping you overcome an obstacle and either created value or additional revenue for your company.

I charge my PAYING clients very good money for results I provide them. They value my expertise. How would they feel to know that I'm giving out that very same advice for free? Not too swell I would imagine. In fact, I hope they don't want to call me demanding refunds! That would be tragic. And for those of you who would say *well I can't afford you* let me share this. People ultimately decide what they value and find a way to pay for it. If my knowledge will help you advance your career or grow your business, then absolutely, there is a value and you have to pay for it. There's a big difference between shooting the breeze and mapping out an entire strategy. I'm no more in control of what you can afford than you are of me. It's not my responsibility. I'm sorry if that sounds harsh, but it's the truth. I run a business and as such, I have expenses. So sorry, you'll have to find someone else.

For those of you out there who can't sleep at night because of situations like this, trust me, I understand how hard it can be to establish a monetary value for your expertise. I really struggled with this in the early days of my business. But you must get over it and make yourself comfortable with doing it. If you don't assign a value, someone else will. And chances are if they are already trying to get it for free, they don't value you very much to pay you fairly. As business professionals, it's up to you to assign a value to your gifts, skills and knowledge. By the time you're done reading this book, not only will you have assigned a value to your knowledge, you'll be quoting it like second nature, and without breaking a sweat.

The most prevalent question I get is *how do you draw the line*? I will go into detail about strategies for drawing the line and finding balance. Deciding the point where you begin to charge is tough, especially if you're just starting out. But your knowledge does have value. You've invested time and money into learning your craft, and it's not fair for people to expect you to give it away for free. Even friends and family need to understand that there are boundaries.

For example, I will no longer advise my friends or family for free. I know I've made some people mad....they'll get over it! I have businesses to run, employees to pay, mortgage to pay, office rent to pay, college tuition, etc., etc., etc. I've told this to friends who have promptly replied "me too, you know I don't have much money". SO WHAT. That means you either have to delay your plans or come up with the money to fund your dreams. Period. Giving away free information all the time is the quickest way to end up evicted or foreclosed on. Put that in proper perspective for a moment.

If you're one of those people having problems drawing the line in the sand, this book is definitely for you. Because of the overwhelming responses, I felt the need to write this book to guide anyone who is in a consultative position, or even those with creative gifts that people call upon all the time, to really become comfortable with valuing themselves and being free to let others

10

know not to disrespect that value. Remember, I'm not saying you can never give away free advice. Just be discerning.

Throughout this book I will be sharing my advice to frequently asked questions, offering strategies on differentiating between and drawing the line between fee and free advice, giving you scenarios of people who are experiencing similar situations (and how they managed it), and give you tips to help ease the conversations with people you have to draw that line with. And I'll share some of my own experiences. Of course the names have been changed to protect the innocent…and to avoid a lawsuit! I have even devoted a chapter to handling brain picking during job interviews. I needed to add this chapter because a lot of people have come to me about how to handle an interview that turns into a quest for a blueprint.

Hopefully this book will teach you how to set the boundaries, determine when free turns to fee, and positioning yourself to be respected as the subject matter expert you are. Then you can pay it forward to empower others to do the same.

Chapter 1
Value Thyself

Beyonce said *If you like it then you better put a ring on it*, well I say *Put a **Price** On It*! As I said in the introduction, you must learn to place a value on yourself or others will do it for you. And you may not like the value they assign! Believe that what you know is valuable. If it wasn't then why are they coming to you to solve their problems? You are their chance to solve a problem or find a solution. That has value. Charge for it and don't be afraid.

You spend a lot of time, money and energy in your professional growth. Between student loans and tuition for college or trade school, the cost of certifications that may not be picked up by your employer, ongoing continuing education in the form of classes, workshops, conferences and seminars, the cost of association membership dues and investments made in coaching and mentoring programs, it's easy to see that you've made significant investments in learning what you know. Why are you just allowing free access to that? Other people are benefitting from your investment. Sure, that can be a good thing, in moderation.

I like to equate their using you to our friendly neighborhood bootleggers. Sure, they want to see the movie and let everyone see the movie for cheap and make a profit in the mean time. This is their way of sticking it to Hollywood. Bootleggers gather the content (illegally) then attempt to resell it to others cheaper under the guise of it being for the people and line their own pockets. This is the same thing. The producers, artists, developers of the work they busted their butts creating the content don't get a dime off of their sweat equity for each product that is sold by a bootlegger. But the one who does no work at all, infringes on that and charges others like they're getting a deal. Remember that next time you buy a bootleg DVD! It's not right.

A lot of time and money goes into producing and filming a movie. Production staff, producers, directors, actors, and so on, get paid for their time. The market (or in this case the studio) assigns a value to the finished product. We see this by the outrageous prices of movie tickets and DVDs. But they must charge to recoup the investment made to create the film. Then you have some local hustler come through and make poor quality copies and sell them for $2 on the street corner. Who does this benefit other than the bootlegger and the seemingly "savvy" shopper who purchased the movie on the cheap? OK maybe this seems like an extreme example and many of you may not get the analogy, so let's try another.

You invest tons of time and money into educating yourself while your neighbor is content with a high school diploma. You're both equally eager to do big things with your life. You share common interests so you talk frequently with one another about your plans and find out you have commonalities. Only, when you share your ideas, the neighbor is taking notes and biding his time to execute YOUR plan. He hasn't done any research, didn't put in any time at all. But he beats you to the punch, thanks to your generosity in sharing what you know, and he becomes a millionaire off YOUR idea. Even though you shared your ideas with him, he takes credit and you get not one thin dime for your troubles. Is it starting to become clear to you?

Now the contrarian would say *"oh well, first mover advantage. All is fair in love and war (and business)"*. And he would be right. He or she who moves first, reaps the rewards (most times). You can't expect that everyone will have a chivalrous attitude as you or I do. This is a dog eat dog world and if you leave yourself open, you'll get eaten up. That's why it's so important to determine not only your value, but also with whom you intend to share your knowledge or skills.

But how do you put a value on what you know? Ah, that's the million-dollar question. It's not always easy to quantify with a dollar amount, but try we must. I know many people, especially women, have a hard time assigning a dollar amount to themselves because it feels uncomfortable. They feel it's crude to say *this is what I'm worth*. But listen, it's not crude. Like I said in the opening chapter, you invest a lot of time and money into your education, formal and otherwise.

When you go for a job, you expect to be paid a certain salary, right? This is no different. I too, was a bright-eyed start-up at one time, so I know how hard it can be to assign a value. But it's really rather simple. In fact, when you're a business owner or independent consultant/contractor, it is important to establish your going rate from the beginning. After all, people are paying you for three things: your unique perspective on a topic, your delivery of that perspective, and the years of experience you've invested in becoming an expert. It's OK to adjust that rate as you become more familiar with and popular on the market.

If you've never thought about assigning a dollar value, let's look at a simple formula. I always tell people to think of a dollar amount they would feel comfortable making each year. For some it's $50K, for others it's $100K and yet others $1 million. It's pretty straight forward to determine your hourly rate if you're an employee. But when you're an independent, the numbers don't add up the same. You have to account for taxes, benefits and incidentals which all come out of your own pocket.

Keep in mind though, depending on what you've done in the past or are currently doing, you can use that to determine what your fees should be. For example, if you're "known" (have written a book that has gotten attention, appeared on a radio or TV show, write for a prominent or visible media outlet or blog, etc.), or you've worked with a list of satisfied clients willing to sing your praise, you can probably start at a higher rate than someone who doesn't have those things under their belt. But don't be discouraged. Everyone has to start somewhere, so don't let other people's success dictate the fees you set for yourself. People will place value where they see value is added regardless of how long you've been at it.

So let's get back to your number. Depending on what you offer, you can establish different fees for different services or information. And you always want to keep the numbers consistent, unless it's that time of year where you are raising your rates. By the way, you should be revisiting your rates every eighteen months to two years and adjusting accordingly. I always advise coming up with a *fee schedule*.

Creating a fee schedule will allow you to have your numbers at your fingertips whenever someone is a potential client and allows people to see the various prices for what you offer. A fee schedule gives you a professional look, plus you're not quoting different rates for different people every time you answer the phone.

Keep your fees as consistent as possible to avoid confusion. A fee schedule is a great filtering tool when people want to pick your brain. When I started handing them out, I noticed people either disappeared or showed me they were serious about engaging me for my expertise. Either way, it helped me cut right to the chase and save what could have been wasted time. It's up to you to decide at what point you whip out that fee schedule.

You have the power to determine if a person is worthy of a discount or waiver of your fee. If you choose to go there, however, then be prepared for future consequences, such as them always expecting a discount. Be clear up front about what you're giving them and why.

So I ask you again, what is your magic number. How much money do you want to earn in a year? Regardless of what your number is, take that number, and divide it by 2080 (the number of hours you would realistically work full time in a year). So if your number is $100K that would be 100,000 /2080=48.08 (rounded up). Now take another 35-45% out for taxes and benefits. That number isn't looking too good, huh? I don't even want to continue on with the math. It's too depressing.

But suffice it to say you're not going to say your time is worth $48 per hour! Especially when you consider the costs you've incurred to gain your knowledge and what that knowledge means to your clients' bottom line. That number will end up in the red. So here's where you take a realistic look at how much you want to make and factor in all of the extras so that when you do the math, it makes sense to you and you end up with a number you're comfortable with. So when you come up with your number, make sure to factor in expenses, taxes, AND PROFIT.

When you find yourself in the position of dispensing

advice, that is the time to stop and say "this is my fee for consulting with you should we go deeper" or "normally, when I consult with a client, this is my fee for the information you're asking". At that point, they'll either take it or leave it. But they will see that you are a serious professional. Now, you may have some…no maybe about it, you will…who will come to you and say "are you serious" and be put off by you informing them of your fees. And that's OK. But you need to take control over the situation and explain to them that there is a premium for your knowledge and you have clients that pay for the very same advice from the very beginning. Pitch it to them as if to say "how would you feel if I charged you, but gave the same information away to the next person who comes through my door?". That usually puts things into perspective for them. And if it doesn't, good riddance.

Be prepared. You will get some angry people who will be offended because you won't give them a freebie. Those are the people you don't want as clients anyway because you'll never convert them to paying clients. Someone who is serious about gaining access to your expertise will have no problem paying for it. It's when you start letting people slide and discounting yourself for everyone, that no one will take you serious. They'll only take advantage. Does everything have to be a business arrangement? No. But most things should be. There is a time and place for charity and philanthropy. But again, YOU dictate those times.

Let me talk a little about philanthropic or volunteer services. I'm not heartless. In fact I've already mentioned that each year I pick several people to either put through one of my programs or help them with consulting for free. That's right, I do.

20

But I do it on my own terms. There's no system or logic to it. It's a spiritual thing. I usually know in my heart when God will give me a sign to help someone out. And I honor that. Most times, they are thankful. Sometimes they feel entitled and expect me to continue way after our time is up.

I don't do it for an ego trip and I don't announce when I do it. I just simply pick people to gift my services to. Now don't think that just because I shared that here in this book that I'll be doing this for everyone. Once again, I run a business and it takes money to run it. So please don't call or email me asking about this. I choose randomly, I don't accept solicitations or queries.

It can be a scary thing, especially for new professionals, to assign a dollar value to yourself or your knowledge. Don't allow fear to dictate how you price your fees. Keep in mind, as you set your fees, you'll weed out the people who weren't going to be clients anyway, and you'll gain clients who'll have a healthy respect for you because you value yourself and are confident in your knowledge. Honorable people will pay for results and quality. All the rest are just window shoppers. That's THEIR issue, not yours. You will find that the crowd thins out the moment you assign a monetary value to your knowledge. Trust me, it's for the best.

Creating a fee schedule may seem like a daunting task, especially if you quote different prices to different people based on your relationships. They are an essential tool for service-based businesses. You should also be using them as a guideline to create packages and bundled services for potential clients. Once you've moved from giving advice to full-fledged consulting or actually providing a service, you must charge, and know what to charge.

Whenever someone wants to pick your brain, make sure you have your fee schedule in front of you. Give them a quote for how much it will cost them. They'll either pay it or move on. If they choose to move on, good riddance to them. They weren't interested in paying you anyway. Let them figure it out on their own. The key is for you not to be upset by it. It's not you, it's them. And if they were going to be so much trouble, you probably dodged a bullet!

Stacy's Story

Stacy is an estate planner building her practice. She regularly sends out an information newsletter, speaks at a variety of events to educate women in financial well being, she shares tips via tweets, Facebook® and Linked In® posts and she has a YouTube® channel. And she recently started using video conferences and teleconferences to host free impromptu sessions to help people get comfortable with investing.

There are three young ladies who follow Stacy and have been for a few years, soaking in all the knowledge she shares. They have mentioned on many occasions that when they *get their money right*, they would hire her to be their financial planner. Lately they had been emailing her asking her how she would handle certain situations. At first, her responses were general and she would also disclaim that she couldn't advise them properly without working with them in an official capacity. They would assure her that it was only a question that was on their minds and that they just needed to know what she would do if in their shoes.

After about six months, Stacy finally got tired of this and asked the ladies to meet with her (individually of course) and they agreed. She wanted to put an end to this knowledge abuse, but didn't know what to say to them. So she called me and told me about the situation. I told her the first thing she needed to do was stop giving away additional free information and start referring people with questions to her many free online resources. Anything beyond that, they would have to schedule an appointment for a consultation to see if they could work together. When she told me about the flurry of questions I stopped her in her tracks. I told her they were using the oldest trick in the book and she had to nip that in the bud immediately.

Let's look at the facts. They keep telling her *when they get their money right* they would hire her. They read, listen to and participate in every free thing she offers. Then on top of that, they ask her "hypothetical" questions? Ray Charles (RIP) could have seen what was going on! They were taking advantage and it needed to stop. But first Stacy had to work on herself so that she could be in a place where she could demand respect for her value.

First I sat down with her to determine her fees. She didn't have a written fee schedule, nor had she categorized the different services. So I had her create a fee schedule. Then we looked at each email and matched them up to the fees. It was an eye opening experience because she realized how much she was losing out on by not charging them. Then I had her sit down and create a consultation policy, complete with a clearly defined policy of when billable hours would kick in with no exceptions. Next, she made a list of things she would offer for free and defined the people for whom and circumstances in which she would offer them. And whenever she did a video, speaking engagement or shared content, she was to end off with a link to her website and an invitation to a personalized consultation with the implication of it leading to a client relationship instead of appearing to offer more free advice.

Stacy felt such relief when we finished. But she was still nervous about her meetings with the ladies. Even though she knew she was worth her fees, she still was hesitant about telling them they'd be cut off from personalized free advice. After all, these women looked up to her. She didn't want to offend them.

Well to put it bluntly, and I did, I told her "how offended would you be if you couldn't make your mortgage payment and they foreclosed on your home? Would the bank understand that you chose to give free advice and didn't feel right collecting money?". And it hit her. She got it. Until then, she hadn't put it all together. She never put herself in a mindset to think about what all that lost revenue could cost her.

When Stacy had the conversations with each of the ladies, two got upset and they didn't "need" her after all if she was going to be nasty about it. Stacy wasn't nasty. In fact she doesn't have a nasty bone in her. She just drew the line and they were upset because they were busted. Instead of admitting their own selfishness and wrong doing, they made themselves feel better by shifting the blame on to Stacy, making her the bad guy.

As for the third woman, she understood. She admitted that in a way, she knew what she was doing and wanted to see how much she could get away with. She wasn't proud of it, but she reasoned when your funds are limited, you have to get what you can whenever, or wherever, you can. She did appreciate Stacy's honesty and respected her business.

Fourteen months later, Stacy took the third woman on as a (paying) client.

So you see, part of the responsibility falls on your shoulders. People will only treat you the way you allow them to treat you. And they will value you only if you value yourself. Don't set out giving away free advice and special one off freebies unless you intend to continue it. And make sure you set limitations. How you condition people (or potential clients) is how they will use that to connect with, communicate and set expectations going forward in your relationship with them. Set good habits in the beginning so you don't find yourself frustrated, overwhelmed and underpaid.

Chapter 2
Draw the Line...Clearly

We all have a bit of humanitarian inside each of us (at least I hope we do). Most humans want to help others. But it becomes a burden when you're trying to solidify your role as a serious professional and everyone expects you to continue shelling out free advice. If you learn nothing else from this book, learn that you have to set your boundaries or you will be taken advantage of. I had to learn this over time, the hard way.

It's perfectly OK to want to give away advice and help people. In fact, remember the quote I opened this book with? Well while I agree with the quote, it can be a double-edged sword. In my humble opinion (OK, maybe not so humble), that quote applies to the *right* kind of people. Yes, there is a difference. You have two types of people in this instance.

The first type is the **habitual picker**. They just want to keep coming back and get as much as they can with little effort and no investment. They want things handed to them or drawn out in a blueprint, and scoff at feeling obligated to pay for it or pay it forward to others. After all, in their mind, nobody *really* helped or gave them anything, so why should they help anyone else. Selfish, huh? They feel entitled and it is *your privilege* to help them. Let's see, if you keep helping this kind of person, and this person has selfish intentions, exactly how will you end up getting what you want? You don't have to be a martyr. I don't think God intended us to feed the egos of the greedy. It is perfectly fine to limit your interaction with or flat out deny helping this kind of person. I certainly wouldn't fault you for it.

The second type of person is the **hopeful** picker. They're the ones who, for whatever reason, don't have the access to resources (human, financial or otherwise) but have a purpose they want to fulfill and a genuine heart. They can't pay you and often feel guilty because they feel they're benefitting so much but don't know how to return the favor. They are extremely appreciative of any help they receive. When they are able, they come back to you and offer to pay you something, or they pay it forward to the next person, without expectation of getting anything in return. They value your knowledge and expertise and have a moral code within themselves. This is the type of person I believe Zig Ziglar was referring to in his quote.

I've had this conversation many times, especially since my article came out. People called me selfish for wanting to draw boundaries, and even cautioned that it would backfire on me and cost me potential clients. But I was OK with that. Each person who really wants to work with me will find a way to make it happen. They know that what I bring to the table will help them solve problems and create measureable results. They respect me enough as a businesswoman and for my craft to not demean me or diminish my value.

I say this to you because I have a sneaking suspicion that you need to hear this. Your knowledge and skills are valuable and deserve to be honored as such. Setting boundaries doesn't mean you're egotistical or narcissistic. Some of you have asked me *but I'm just starting out in my career/business. Who am I to put a price on my knowledge, especially when knowledge is free on the Internet?* To that I respond HAH! You **are** worthy, you are entitled and don't you ever think differently.

It doesn't matter if you have two years of experience or twenty. You are worthy and don't let anyone tell you otherwise, or try to capitalize on your insecurity or relatively new experience. Even a doctor just graduating medical school has a right to earn pay for his work. Tenure is the other person's hang up, not yours. And you shouldn't be made to feel guilty about or apologize for it. The difference between you and someone with twenty years of experience is the world doesn't know you yet. Deliver great value and service, and you'll be sought after by the masses.

Yes, there is free information all over the Internet. Most of it is purposely free. But *application* and *implementation* of said information is **not**. Someone has to do the work. You can watch a video on YouTube about how to change out your plumbing. But unless you're a handy person (man or woman), someone has to do the actual work for the desired results. If it's not going to be you, it has to be someone. So while you may get the *know how* from a free video, you have to get someone to do the work, and I bet my last dollar that the person you get won't be doing it for free. And here's a little secret. People purposely put free information on the web to bait you. They will share the *why* and the *what*, but not the **how**. Make sure you pay attention to that last line because it's going to be explained later on.

So what should you share for free? That's a good question. It depends on your comfort level and your expertise. It also depends on the value you assign to it. For example, in my previous life (I love the way that sounds!) I was a Recruiter. I made my money by finding the right talent for the clients that hired me. That meant devising a strategy, creating a marketing plan, filtering through candidates, interviewing people, collaborating with hiring managers, negotiating salaries and ultimately closing the deal. Let's focus on the strategy part.

In recruiting, strategy is half the battle. I spent time researching where ideal candidates were and making sure I got myself in front of them so I could (in a sense) sell my client to them. For those of you who believe recruiting is just putting up some ads, looking at some resumes and making offers, grow up! It's never that simple when you're looking for REAL talent. I put a lot of time into strategy, depending on the type of job and level of complexity in filling it so I could have a better chance of finding the right talent. So you can understand when someone, another recruiter, comes to me and asks me for some strategies on finding talent, I get tight-lipped.

They want me to map it all out for them so they don't have to do the grunt work. But I get paid for the grunt work, so why should I share those strategies? I shouldn't. Consider those my trade secrets that are not readily available to the world. Are they strategies that perhaps other recruiters use? They sure are. But each recruiter has their own variation of what works for them, and what works for me is not up for grabs or discussion.

What I can share, however, is my opinion on processes, tools, and even recruiting styles. I will make those available freely all day every day. My opinion doesn't mean that it will affect the outcome one way or another. It merely means what I would or wouldn't do for my own situation. Anything that is freely available on the web is open for discussion. But when implementation of said information becomes a conversation, I have to switch into consultant role because now you're asking me to form a specific strategy for you to use. That's consulting, not advising.

I speak at events where I get tons of people who come up

to me immediately after my panel wanting advice. Sometimes they'll ask me one or two general questions, to which I will give a broad answer. But when they want to monopolize my time to examine a critical problem they're facing, I have to shut it down and recommend that they schedule a *consultation* at another time. Did you see what I just did? I just turned the conversation into a potential business opportunity with the use of one word.

Using that one word, *consultation,* let's people know where you stand and how they can move forward with you. It's a word that so many people forget to use and it costs them valuable time and potential dollars. Think about it and let's look at an example.

Let's say you're a Wordpress expert. You can create sites in your sleep, you are up on the latest and greatest plugins and widgets. You know how to code like nobody's business and you're always sharing the latest finds with your audience, friends, family, colleagues, etc. You speak on a panel about the benefits of moving a website to the Wordpress platform. People are furiously scribbling notes and nodding in agreement with many of your key points. At the end of your panel, a swarm of people rush up to you and start asking a range of questions.

The first person asks you for widgets and plugins you'd recommend using for various purposes. You share this information freely because after all, it is available on the Internet. The next person shares that they aren't very tech savvy and she doesn't feel confident in installing these widgets and plugins. Since you already told her where to find them couldn't you just do it for her? Stop. What is your next step? Hell, what is your next thought? Well if you're me, you would tell her that you'd be happy to set up a *consultation* with her at another time so you can sit down and evaluate whether or not you could help her and to what degree. Then you'd follow up with "my usual charge for that is $xx.xx" then you step back and wait on her reply. She'll either accept or walk away. Her action is dependent on the words that come out of your mouth.

We train people in what to expect from us from the time we first engage them. So it's important to set those guidelines from the very beginning so you don't feel caught or trapped. That second conversation could have gone a totally different way. In fact I'm sure it has for some of you. Let me lay out for you how that particular conversation turns into a brain picking session.

You: *Well, it's really very simple. If you would just go to this website, download this plugin, then program it, you'll be up and running in a snap.*

Brain Picker: *No, I'm telling you, I'm not tech savvy. I know for you it may be easy. But for me, not so much. Can you just take a look at my site now? I have my iPad with me.*

You: *Well, I really am pressed for time. But you know what, let me finish up here and meet you outside. I hate to see people suffering over something that's really quite simple.*

Brain Picker: *OK, I'll meet you outside.*

Then you walk outside to find her, laptop fully charged, saving a seat for you with a look on her face that says *you're my savior.* You look at the website, show her a few plugins, download them for her and install them to her site because after all, it only takes you 10-15 minutes tops. No big deal. She is already so distressed. An hour goes by, you've installed her plugins, set them, gave her a mini-tutorial and she has a newly updated website...from the work you did for her...for FREE.

Do you see how that got messy very quickly? Do you see where this person went wrong? Most times the brain picker will reason with you that because of their incompetence with your expertise her problems will be solved with just a few questions and some of your time and patience. You can actually substitute any scenario for the one above. Most times we feel like it's quicker to just do it ourselves instead of trying to explain it to people. And that costs us time and money. The sad part is most brain pickers know this and they make a play on that.

You have to learn how and when to draw the line. As I mentioned above, knowing when to turn a conversation into a consultation is to your advantage. The longer you let things coast along, the more likely you are to get fleeced of your time and deserved dollars. If someone asks you to meet with them to help them with a problem or for advice, ask questions before making a commitment. The answers to these questions will allow you to determine if there is a need to proceed or refer them elsewhere. Here are some questions you should be asking during the first phase, which is the qualifying stage:

Do you need advice or are you looking for help or a solution? There is a big difference. Asking for advice is similar to getting your opinion on how you would handle a situation. It's not asking a person to map out a step-by-step plan to solve a problem. You have to determine what they mean in the opening so that you know what the logical next step should be. Pay attention to what they are telling you and asking of you. When they start talking about "I just need someone to..." be very careful. In their mind, they just need a quick, simple fix that shouldn't take too much of *your* time. This means they just want you to tell them what's wrong and how to fix it so they won't need you. Don't do it!

If you're looking for help or a solution, what have you tried on your own, and who have you contacted for assistance? Now let's stop here for a second because their answer could be considered a loaded one. Perhaps the person innocently doesn't know where to turn for help on this matter. So it's only logical that you might be the first person they've reached out to. In this case, you have to tread carefully. Ask them why they sought you out and listen to their responses. If they say something like "*I notice you give a lot of advice on Twitter or Facebook and thought you could help me*" you need to set the record straight. Let them know that yes, you do give out tips, but they are general in nature and that true clients would benefit from a consultation and a plan of action they can put in place. Then you explain that there is a cost for that. If they mention they've checked out a few people but wanted to check you out based on your tweets, interviews, writing, etc., proceed with caution. They might be looking for freebies, and not really looking to invest in solutions.

Have you set aside a budget specifically to solve this issue? This is the *gotcha* question. You have to be prepared to walk away at this point. I don't care how much you need the *business*, don't waiver. If someone is serious about working with you and really needs your help, they will either already have planned for this expense or will realize the value and make room in the budget for it. Unfortunately, this is a screening out question and many brain pickers will run to the nearest exit the moment the word budget comes out of your mouth. I've seen it many times. When I ask the budget question, the first thing out of their mouth is *well I only needed you to answer one question* or *I only needed this one problem fixed.* To that I responded *well this is what it costs to work with me and if you don't have a budget, perhaps you should consider working with someone else, or I can refer you elsewhere.* Don't spend too much time going back and forth because ultimately they will not become a paying client if they can't come up with the budget.

How do you think I/my company/my services can be of help to you? This is another one of those sit back and listen type questions. Much like the question above (about solutions and other people they've turned to), this is used as a way to screen out. Now playing devil's advocate, some people don't quite know how to articulate themselves. So they may very well not know how to say what they mean or need. Pay attention to their tone and intention. If they are well meaning and honestly seem to have no other place to turn, chances are they just need to be pointed in the right direction. You can potentially turn them into a client by asking the right questions and getting them to tell you exactly what they need. On the flip side, once again, look out for the person that says *oh I just need you to answer a few questions.* Don't waste more than five minutes on this question. Otherwise you'll find yourself playing a clever game of pick my brain, with the other person playing you like a chess game to see how much free information they can get from you.

How soon can you realistically, according to your

budget, hire someone to work on this? By now you've just about qualified them because they should (by now) know that there will be a cost to work with you. In their mind, they are probably trying to run the numbers to see if they can engage you. If they end the conversation here or tell you to let them get back to their office and think about it, they're probably not interested in paying. In fact, some of them will be resentful that you've been asking them all of these questions. But stick to your guns. Qualifying people is the only way to save your sanity and cut down on brain picking.

When are you free for a consultation to discuss further? This is the jackpot question. If after all of the above, they are ready to sit down and have a conversation with you, a professional conversation, there is a high probability that they will sign on as a client. Now don't be fooled. They could just be going through the motions just to see how much they can get out of you. Hey, some people will try that last ditch effort to see how much they can get and how far they can go. Stand firm and keep it professional. Once you've gotten through the questions, be prepared to schedule an appointment. With all of the smart phones and tablets out there, you have no excuse to not set something up on the spot. Pull out that phone or tablet and get a commitment on the calendar.

I will admit, this is going to take some practice. You may think asking all of these questions is a bit much. But trust me, once you get some experience under your belt, you'll be more comfortable and thankful. You'll save a lot of time and you'll pick up real, legitimate clients. Practice on friends and family first. Since they are often the worst offenders, they will be perfect to practice on. Don't *tell* them you're practicing on them. That takes the learning out of it. Instead, just defer to the list of questions the moment they begin asking for advice or freebies. Observe and document their reactions and responses.

Also pay attention to your own performance. Some of you might be on the shy side or may feel funny about setting boundaries because you're still kind of new in the industry. As I've said before, get over it! People will treat you as you allow them to treat you and they will assign *their* perceived value of you based on how you carry yourself. The more confident you are, the more likely people are to take you seriously. This is not the time to cower or shrink back.

Before you can feel comfortable having these conversations with people, you must find the confidence to not just set your rates, but accept them and be comfortable with them. If you quote a rate and then apologize for or rationalize the rate, you're guaranteed to get taken and lose your leverage. People can smell fear. If they see that you can be negotiated down or that you feel so bad that they cannot afford you, they will play on that.

So take time to really sit and assign the proper rates to your services. Then practice saying them out loud to others. Don't ask if they think the rates are fair or how they would act if you told them the rates. Just tell them the rates and sit back. The silence will be awkward, but stand strong and confident.

Before you can set boundaries you have to be clear and comfortable with those boundaries. You are a professional with knowledge and expertise that you've spent time, money and energy developing. You are well within your right to give free advice and help others. I recommend it. But know where to draw the line and don't let people take advantage of you.

Adrienne's Story

As a recruiter, I'm often compared with other recruiting firms when I sit down with a client. I always get calls asking about how we work, what's involved and what we charge. More times than not, I'll get the dreaded "but XYZ company only charges this much". It's very irritating because I'm not in business to compete with other companies' prices. I provide a value and results and should be judged on that alone.

Remember earlier in this chapter I said to be mindful of doing business with friends and family, as they are the worst offenders when it comes to wanting freebies or the hook up? Well one day a friend of mine called me up and told me she wanted to work with me. At first I thought great, because she had a successful business that always seemed to keep busy. She had confided in me that she hadn't had much luck in finding talent and that other search firms were not giving her the results she needed. She threw in some compliments and mentioned how proud she was of me. Then she went in for the kill.

"Listen, we're friends so I know you won't gouge me. I need two software developers like yesterday but I can only afford to pay them about $45,000 each". I thought OK, perhaps I can get her some more junior developers who had great potential. She balked at that and said she needed someone with 5-7 years of experience. I said to her "are you kidding me? Have you done comps on the salary?" to which she replied "no I haven't, can you do that for me?". Now being that she was a friend, I said sure and threw in the research before even getting a contract in place. I gathered the data and sent her some pretty in depth information supporting salaries that I had suggested. While she wasn't too thrilled, she agreed. At that point, I had done too much and it was my fault for throwing it in before signing on the dotted line.

When it came time to discuss terms and execute a contract, this same friend got upset with me because I had to adjust my fee based on the new salaries. For those who don't know, recruitment firms get paid by percentage of the first year's total compensation per hire. Being a friend, I not only gave her a reduced fee (10% lower than my standard), I also set the fee at the base annual salary, not total compensation. Well she did not like that. It was more than she'd wanted to pay. When I pointed out the time I had already invested by doing the comps and preparing a report for her, she feigned ignorance. I only usually do that after a contract is signed and I did that as a favor to her.

Next up was negotiating terms. She wanted me to work like other firms she'd worked with before. After all, they allowed her to be flexible with the payment terms. Here I am thinking, *this chick has a $50 million company and she's haggling with me over terms?* My terms are iron clad for recruiting. I get one-third as retainer upon signing the contract, one-third when an offer is accepted and one-third 90 days after the start date. She wanted me to allow her to pay half after the person was hired and half 90 days after the start date.

As you can imagine, I didn't work with her. I still love her though! When you work with friends, they tend to take advantage and use the friendship card as leverage to get a better deal. Now they know that they would never haggle or bargain with their own clients, but it doesn't dawn on them that the rules don't change simply because they're on the other side of the table. I was angry with her for a long time after that. It wasn't because I lost a sale (they are plentiful). It was because she didn't respect me enough as a businesswoman to understand and respect my company policies. In my eyes, she didn't take me serious even though I have been highly recognized in the recruiting industry and have worked with many powerhouse brands that didn't have any problems with my policies. And I always delivered stellar results.

So be careful when you choose to do business with or favors for friends and family. They will take advantage the quickest and not think twice about it. After all, it's you, and you all go way back. They should be entitled to a freebie or a hook up every now and then, right? NEXT!

Chapter 3
*Free Lunch My A**, Beware of the Signs*

OK, I know you've probably read my Forbes article (have I plugged that enough yet?). And no doubt, you saw that infamous line about the *turkey sandwich*. It still cracks me up! I still have people emailing me asking if they added a salad or chips to that sandwich would I consider meeting with them. LOL is usually my answer. But I digress. As you can pretty much gather, that line had nothing to do with an actual turkey sandwich as much as it had to do with the symbolism of it.

Before I get into that, let's go back to the root of where I think this problem starts. Networking has really upped the ante for brain pickers. Now I know what you're going to say. *But Adrienne, you're Ms. Networking Diva. You're always telling people they should network their asses off. That was you, wasn't it?* Yes, it was and still is me. I stand by my belief that you must network to be successful. Without it, no one person's career or business can survive (let alone thrive) very long.

There is no problem with networking in theory. In fact, hopefully you've read my two books *Go Ahead, Talk to Strangers: The Modern Girl's Guide to Fearless Networking* or *Fearless Networking Without Asking Permission*. And if you haven't, why not? Go to my website **www.empowerme.org** (or Amazon) to get them. In these books I walk the reader through best practices and tips they can use as their own to build a solid network and get comfortable with the idea of mutually beneficial networks. Ah, they key phrase here is *mutually beneficial*.

The fact is that while social media and social networking has made it easier for the shy or introverted to break into networking, it has also produced a bunch of ill informed, selfish people who don't know how to do it the right way. By the logic of most people, as long as we're connected online in some way, or know the same people, it means we have an actual relationship. This is such a common misconception and just outright wrong. Networking of any type takes interaction on and offline to build a trusting relationship. If you can't master that first, you have a problem. Social networking has made the inhibited uninhibited, and the greedy greedier. And it's made people feel entitled because they "know" you.

I'm no psychologist (I'm a recruiter, which is the next best thing...HAH) but for me to be inclined to help you (for fee or for free) I need to get to know and understand who you are and what your true needs are. I can't do that through a series of tweets or status updates. Because I'm somewhat of a pubic figure (*watch out Oprah, I'm gaining on you!*), people feel they already *know* me, but it puts me at a disadvantage because most times I don't know them.

When they listen to me on air, or see me on TV or read my writing, they feel a closeness to me. Because they know many of my thoughts and laugh at my snarky comments or engage in lengthy conversation via tweets or status updates, they feel comfortable approaching me. I have no problem with that because I want to remain as accessible as I can if it will serve to help others. The problem comes when they feel that because we're *networking* and I should be familiar with them, I should give them free information or help at their discretion.

Let the record show, I take full responsibility for conditioning people to believe this. It's because I am all over the web (or at least my advice) people feel that as a natural extension of that, I should be helping them for free. I've painted myself into that and I am working on it. I've gotten a lot better at it, but I still have my moments. People email and call me all the time asking to take me to lunch so they can pick my brain, but I often remark (only half joking) can't we just shoot the breeze? I try to set the tone from the very beginning so there are no problems or hurt feelings.

When someone asks you to lunch, you have to get to the heart of their true intentions before you accept. Remember in the last chapter when we talked about the set of questions you should ask to qualify a potential client? Well the same applies in this situation. It's very easy to get caught up in a phone conversation and get roped into joining someone for lunch. If time is money in your business, and I'm guessing it is, it is important that you vet these calls in advance. No, don't tell you assistant to grill them with a bunch of rude questions. Politely let them know that you are up against some major deadlines for projects and your time is limited.

Ask if there is a specific question you can answer on the phone that might help them. If they still insist on meeting you, ask can they come to your office or a location closer to you at your convenience. The answer may surprise you. In some instances, they'll be put off by the thought of being inconvenienced themselves, that they say never mind. But if a person is serious about meeting you, they will do it on your terms. Another method that works for me is giving them an outrageous time to meet. I know one high-powered executive who tells people to meet her at 6AM. She said that's how she knows when someone is serious.

If someone is inviting you to lunch, it stands to reason

that they will also be paying. Don't get your knickers in a knot. I don't require people to buy me lunch. In fact, a number of rude people have invited me and then asked the waiter for separate checks. Talk about having no Vaseline! (OK that was a bit crass even for me, but you get my point). On the flip side of that, I've had people ask to meet me at Starbuck (my favorite escape) only to buy me a cup of tea. But what they want from me is worth way more than that tea and they've co-opted time that could have been spent with paying clients. I got nothing out if the encounter but tea and conversation. And it wasn't really a conversation because I didn't get any questions answered nor did I get anything of value in return for my time. Where's the tradeoff or incentive for me?

There is no such thing as a free lunch. Something is always being traded. Gas for your car, time away from your work, giving away valuable information, and energy are all prices that are often paid even if there is no money exchanged. Am I advocating that we all start breaking out the calculator each time someone calls you to go to lunch? Of course not. But I am telling you that nothing is free or without some kind of string attached. And let's go beyond that. A phone or Skype call costs. You still have to pay your provider for your phone or Internet service. You still invested time and money into honing your craft. Somewhere, somehow you had to fork over time and money to get you to the level of expertise you're at today. Like it or not, it's a fact.

So how do you deal with the dreaded and somewhat uncomfortable coffee/lunch/breakfast/drinks question? I'll tell you how. By creating a vetting strategy that works best for you. Much like I said in the last chapter, you have to screen people from the get go. You cannot feel guilty about it. Don't set yourself so far above the masses that you're obnoxious about it. But make sure people are respectful of your time and obligations. Decide what kind of calls and invitations you will accept or not accept. Are there certain situations were you would sit down with someone and willingly help them with a free consultation? And if so, how much information do you share and how far are you willing to take it? Are you going to turn friends and family away as a rule? What about up and coming professionals? Will you give them the benefit of your knowledge gratis to steer them in the right direction? All of these variables have to be taken into account.

When you are the holder of the skills or knowledge, people want to bargain with you. Sometimes they have excellent bargaining chips, sometimes they don't. Perhaps they cannot pay you in money but can make incredible connections for you. Or maybe they have some service or product that they can exchange for your knowledge. You never know what they bring to the table unless you ask. The problem with many professionals is they automatically assume the other person is just looking to pick their brain (OK, maybe *some* are) and they don't use this as an opportunity to turn it into a win-win for both of you. In Chapter 6 I'll get into more detail about this even exchange concept.

For now, you should be vetting people before saying yes to meeting them. Be warned, not all meetings will be fruitful. It's a chance you take, but you need to set the tone and draw the boundaries. If you're the type of person who prefers to keep it strictly professional, decline lunch/coffee invitations unless they are strictly non-business. I know that sounds confusing, but it's not. Some people just like to keep the two separate to avoid any conflict. That's a smart thing to do, especially if you're an in demand professional. Don't be afraid to let people know that you prefer to unwind during such occasions and you are off the clock on all things business. They have no choice but to respect it.

Keep in mind, sometimes they will attempt to steer the conversation towards business (sneaky little devils!). If the conversation swings around to business, quickly and politely tell them you're off the clock. If they are interested in a consult they can book an appointment and let them know what the charge is for that. A true professional will understand and honor that. But be warned, the serious brain picker will not like that, and he or she will continue to push the boundaries. Stand firm and shut it down if it comes to that. I've had this happen on occasion.

My favorite is the person who understands we are out socially, not professionally, and they will go overboard on the compliments hoping to get me to slip up and share my secrets of success in a particular area. In fact, true story, I have a dear friend who told me she was so good at it, I couldn't tell when she was doing it to me. You want to know the funny part? I knew she was doing it, when she was doing it, and as I was giving her the rah, rah inspirational you can do it speech, I was sure to speak to the why and the what, but not the how. Remember, I mentioned that in the last chapter. When you encounter someone who is just relentless in their pursuit of your brain, always give them the *why* and the *what*, but never the *how*. The *how* is how you make your money and don't ever forget it.

If you choose to still accept every invitation, nobody will judge you. But keep in mind, you train people to have certain expectations of you. So don't get mad when you find certain people keep coming back over and over. It's perfectly fine to give away as much information as you are comfortable sharing. But keep in mind, you run a business and your bills can't be paid in sandwiches or coffee. Your creditors will not care that someone did not pay you yet so you can't pay them.

In fact, I'll share a true story. I had a creditor who allowed me to order on terms. I was expecting a particular person to turn into a paying client so I went ahead an ordered my merchandise with the expectation of having the funds to pay it. Well this person kept dragging out meeting after meeting. Unsure of what she really wanted and needed more information from me to make a decision. Finally I caught on and said *look, if you want to become a client we have to make this official. We've invested so much time to this point, it makes sense to move to the next logical step and work together.*

Well she told me she was not in a financial situation to become a client and that I should try her back in the fall. WTF!!!! Not only did I lose out on revenue because I could have been spending that time cultivating *real* clients, but my vendor was pissed at me. I didn't have the money and told her upfront. She said she sympathized with me but she wasn't my bank. At first I was pissed off. But as I thought about it from a business perspective, she was absolutely right. I learned my lesson about brain picking that day, and ever since, I protect myself.

There is no amount of pleasantries, well meaning deeds, kind gestures or sandwiches that will pay your bills. You are not responsible for other people's situations. Yes, we are all obligated to give back in some way. But not when it comes at the expense of your well being. You have to protect your reputation. For the small business, their knowledge is often the life's blood of the business. If you part with it too often without compensation, or allow other people to assign less than fair value to it, you will find yourself on the unemployment line quick, fast, in a hurry.

You call the shots. You assign the value. You create the rules of engagement. Stick to them and make others honor them as well.

Donna's Story

Donna was a brand new entrepreneur. After years in the corporate rat race, she finally decided to strike out on her own and start a Project Management Consultancy. She had gained a lot of respect in her industry and invested a lot of time, money and energy into educating and certifying herself. She has worked on countless project and always with spectacular results. So why shouldn't she go on her own? There were rumors that major lay-offs were on the horizon and she needed to get a Plan B. So she did. But her accomplishments and accolades didn't translate immediately to new business.

While Donna was not new to the industry, she was new to the business world, and people took note (and advantage) of that. From business owners who tried to undercut her prices at every turn (because they threatened to in house the solutions for cheaper) to peers who were envious of her break from the 9-5, Donna couldn't catch a break. She felt that in order to get ahead, perhaps she should start giving away information just to prove she was worthy of the fees she charged.

One day, Donna sat down with a friend and asked her what she was doing wrong. Her first mistake was going to someone who wasn't as successful or more successful than she was. The well-meaning friend told her the Zig Ziglar quote about helping people but she failed to qualify it. She instilled in Donna that in order to be taken serious and to prove her ability, it was just a given that she give away as much information as she could. That was the only way, the friend reasoned, to pay her dues.

And so it began. Donna began attending networking events, spoke for free on panels, shared lots of juicy tips with her social networking community (in fact enough to rival teaching an actual class), and was that go to woman the media loved to contact for a sound bite. She was rarely considered for a featured story, but when they needed a one liner, they called on her. As she became more popular, more people started to take notice. She was contacted by curious people who wanted to know how they could make that jump to entrepreneurship. She was contacted by companies who read about her and wanted her to answer a few quick project management questions to get them on track. She was invited to so many coffee and lunch appointments that all she needed to do was make sure she had dinner at home because that's the only meal she had to supply for herself. Donna was finding her rhythm, or so she thought.

But Donna wasn't happy. Her bills were falling behind. She was running low on her reserve money. Her one major client had some financial difficulties so they informed her that her contract was expiring at the end of the month and wouldn't be renewed. She was in a panic. She had no steady income. But wait, she had a brilliant idea! People really loved her, they loved the information she shared so they appointed her the expert. Why not capitalize on that? So she called up some people who had been struggling and asked to meet them for lunch. After all, when they were in need, she met with them. And she even offered to pay.

One by one, they all made excuses. Times were tough and they didn't have the budget, but all her advice had really been helpful to them. They've implemented her tips and were on the road to recovery. Some decided that in house was the way to go, so there really was no need to waste any more of her time. Out of courtesy to her, they would revisit in six month. Six month came and went, and they never returned her call. What happened to all of these people who were just in love with her expertise? They *needed* her, right?

So Donna came up with Plan B. She decided to hold a class. Actually, a webinar to get as many people as possible on so she could make a nice profit. After all, she heard from some Internet Marketing guru that holding calls and webinars were excellent ways to make money. But she was supposed to make the webinar free and plug her real training through the webinar, giving them the why and the what, but not the how. Donna wasn't a seller and didn't feel comfortable doing that to people, so she spent weeks creating a program and set the fee at $199. And if they wanted additional information, they could sign up to work with her one on one. Brilliant idea! It was…except nobody wanted to pay for it. After all, webinars are supposed to be free. They all are. Why pay her for something they could look up for free on the web?

By this point Donna was desperate. She sat down and went over and over it in her head. People loved her, respected her expertise, so where did everyone go? Didn't her friend tell her if you help enough people you'll eventually get what you need? She simply could not understand. She was always gracious. She met any and everyone for lunch. She always gave helpful advice because she felt like other people merely dangled bait to get a sale. She wanted people to trust her as an authority. But why didn't anyone want to work with her?

BECAUSE OF FREE LUNCHES!

Unfortunately, Donna painted herself in that corner as many of us do. We're so intent on being that go to person, the one who wants to make nice with everyone, the one who never says no. When you fail to set boundaries, you end up failing at your business. Donna didn't have a strategy in place. She didn't learn how to say no or differentiate between fee and free. Sure, she had a fee schedule and she was confident in her rates. But she couldn't get anyone to pay for what she had already given up for free. Her usefulness was over. She had become a commodity in the worst way.

When you start meeting people in a casual setting (coffee or lunch) and provide them with the answers to all of their questions, they'll continue to expect that. Once you open that floodgate, it's hard to reverse course. It's not impossible, but it is extremely difficult. Start out the right way by training people to accept your policies and boundaries. There is no such thing as a free lunch because it will end up costing **you** in the end. Learn to separate business and pleasure and if the lines blur, be ready for a plan to convert the brain picker into a paying client or move on.

Chapter 4
Socializing is Not Consulting and Vice Versa

Undoubtedly, you have at some point been approached by well-meaning (and some self-serving) people asking to take you out to lunch or to meet for coffee as we've covered in the last chapter. I told you to learn how to differentiate between the two. Some times, our personalities endear us to people and the feel like they know us and trust us already, before even getting to know us. That's a dangerous position to be in. Since I talked about this in the last chapter, I'll switch gears a little bit and show you how to draw the line and not let it blur.

You have to keep things light for your own sake (and sanity). I know it's hard when you want to be accepted and respected for your expertise. There's a natural tendency to try to give as much as you can. On the other end of the spectrum, ego can make us start spilling our guts like a turned mob informant. You know the type. *How dare someone doubt my smarts. I'll show them. Once they see how smart I am, they'll beg to work with me.* Yeah...OK. That'll teach **them**. LOL

Some of you will probably cave and throw a few nuggets out there. If you do (I hope you don't), keep it general. Give the why and what but never the how. Anything beyond the why and what comes with a charge. I know I keep harping on this *why, what, how* formula but I think it's important that you understand it and how to best use it. And don't you dare even point them in the direction to obtain the how. That's short changing yourself.

Sometimes I'll get so frustrated because I'm so busy, that it's natural for me.to say *just do this*. But I've trained myself to stop doing that. I'm not trying to cheat myself out of any money. In fact, when I feel those urges coming on, I will recommend to a strategic partner or associate for which I will earn a referral fee.

Hey, don't judge me. Business is business.

But back to socializing. On sites like Twitter, Facebook, Google+ or Linked In, we tend to over share. Yes, I can be a victim of TMI myself on occasion. You get so caught up in the flow of the conversation, that you forget that people are taking notes. Stop that! How many of you have seen those tweet chats each week where a bunch of experts come together to share their expertise with followers in the form of a Q & A type Twitter chat?

Well many are selflessly sharing tips. Some are ego stroking. Hey, it is what it is. They try to one up everyone else with what they perceive as the best or better answer, all the while solidifying themselves as the undisputed expert, while at the same time giving away tons of content that could have been used to turn a passive watcher into a paying client. Now they don't need you because they've gotten all the information they need. What went wrong here?

Socializing has its time and place, online and off. It is important that when you choose to socialize online, you keep it strictly social until the time comes to take it offline. You'll know when it's time to switch to business mode because the questions and the direction of the conversation will change. You should be picking up these cues and planning accordingly. But you shouldn't try to force it. If people only want to engage with you because of your quirky sense of humor or you share the coolest articles or news from the web, you cannot get angry if they don't want to do business. Other people have boundaries too, and you have to respect them.

Lots of people use social media to push their businesses,

and it's a given. But some actually use it to converse, socialize and escape their day to day. They don't appreciate being sold to every minute. But yet, there you have DMs, tweets, private messages, status posts all pushing some kind of product, service, class, call, coaching, or whatever. That gets annoying when you're on the receiving end. So know when to turn it on and especially when to turn it off. I don't want this to become a social media lesson, because this topic goes way beyond just online interaction. But it does set the foundation for offline interaction.

When you decide to meet up with some of your compadres from the Internet, make sure you know up front what you're dealing with. Don't get caught like I did once, when someone I had communicated with for a good deal of time online, invited me to join her and some buddies for drinks. I was excited because I always like to meet people offline and put some reality to the relationship.

Well this particular time, she had me meeting with her and six of her buddies. What I didn't know was that these *buddies* were recruiters. She had talked me up to them and told them about how much she enjoyed my blog and my no-nonsense style. She told them how my writing kept her laughing, but she always learned something from me. Of course, I was flattered. But I was about to be blindsided!

So I walk into the restaurant, laid back and relaxed, ready to have a great time. I think it was game night at this establishment and I was ready to rock. So in I walk and found the group. My networking buddy introduced me to the group and gave them an intro that made me do a double take because I could hardly believe it was me she was talking about. But I graciously said thank you and sat down. The evening started off very well. Everyone chit chatting and getting to know one another. Then the boom dropped.

My networking buddy asked everyone what they thought about my latest blog post. I had written it after something had set me off (which is how some of my blogs are done) and I had hit the nail on the head. Some would argue it was my best post to date, next to the brain picking one, but I digress. So the first questions started with what lead me to write the post. And from that point on, notepads and pens were out and the questions were flying.

About ten minutes into the conversation I started getting a little annoyed. But I help my composure. I had asked a few times who wanted to let the game moderator know that our table wanted to play. But they kept brushing it off and focusing on asking me more questions. Then they started asking specific process related questions that would require me to charge.

My first warning was a half laughing warning that anything further, and I'd have to charge them. They didn't take me serious. Then I started answering their questions with questions. It confused and annoyed them a bit. Then I had to put an end to it. As politely as I could, I told them that they were asking me about stuff my clients pay me for.

I was all for sharing and the sisterhood that is recruiting, but I had to change the subject. After all, we were out to have fun. And I really wanted to play those trivia games. The next thing I know, some of the ladies got an attitude. It wasn't overt, but I could sense it. Since I didn't want to give them a blueprint, they suddenly didn't find me such a hoot any more. A couple of the ladies felt the tension too but tried to bring some levity. By this time, it was time for me to go. I don't like drama, negativity or setups.

The next day I called this networking buddy and told her she really should have warned me about what I was about to walk into. I didn't intend to host a Q & A right there in the middle of a restaurant. She apologized but told me it was my own fault. I should have shut it down when I saw where it was going. I sat for a second to gather my thoughts (really to not curse her out) before I responded. Then I told her that I have no problem giving advice on occasion. I have no problem that my advice is readily available through my blogs, show, articles, posts, etc. But what I did have a problem with was being ambushed on what I thought was a hang out.

Needless to say, that little circle shared how *uncooperative* I was and any chance at hiring any of them as clients was quickly squashed. In a sense, I did do it to myself. I set the tone. I didn't set the proper expectations. Would they have ultimately become clients? I'll never know. But the fact that they felt I owed them anything was insulting at best. And it's not like I never got another client ever again in life. Just not *those* clients. Their loss, not mines.

Learn a lesson from my story. When you build a brand or a reputation, you have to be careful. People will love you as long as you give them what they want whenever they want for free. The moment you try to pull back a bit, they get upset. Are they justified? Perhaps. If you've already programmed them a certain way, you can't just change up half way in. It's like building a free community like Facebook and letting people do and say whatever they want. Then, five years in you announce *hey people we're charging you to use Facebook*, and you have a mass exodus. It's not fair to them and it's not fair to you.

While I agree that you have to mix a little bit of social with business, you have to know when to separate the two. When you're building your brand, you have to determine what you'll share for free, how often and with whom. Know your limits and theirs. When you see people pushing at the boundaries, it's time to either nip it in the bud, or move them over to the qualifying phase. Don't start shouting how your knowledge is how you make your money because frankly, they don't care and aren't supposed to. If you keep letting them blur the lines between social and business, then you have nobody to blame but yourself if you don't correct them.

When you accept social invites, please be sure to clarify that you are going to have fun. You won't be there to talk business. Let them know what your business hours are and what topics are off limits. Always default to a consultation at a later time. Some people may keep pushing, as I mentioned above. But enforce your rules. Push back as much as they push you until they get it. You don't have to pull a Teresa from Real Housewives of New Jersey and flip a table to make your point. But be firm, be quick and be serious. Then move on to the next topic. They'll either respect you for it or hold a grudge. Either way, it's not your problem.

I don't know about you, but when I go out, I go to enjoy myself. I leave work at the office and expect to be able to have fun in peace. I hate being put on the spot, especially in front of a crowd. In a one on one setting, it's more manageable, even if not fully acceptable. But I don't appreciate being thrust into the spotlight to *dance* for people. It's kind of like being a doctor and being asked a cocktail party to take a look at a mole on someone's back. It's totally inappropriate and rude.

Tony's Story

Tony is the sweetest, most humble guy you ever want to meet. He has an uber successful business, and a heart of gold. He does a lot of philanthropic work for the community that he hardly speaks of. He's humble and very low key and never told anyone about his "job". So it was never a shock when people invite him out to lunch or other social gatherings. He's just that kind of guy that everyone wanted to hang out with.

Tony had done many great volunteer projects and for the first time, decided to use his company name to complete a big philanthropic project. Unknown to him, the media was informed and Tony's company along with several other businesses, got some well deserved recognition. When the story aired, people put two and two together and figured out that their Tony, the fun guy, was actually the head of a major company. Every job seeker, vendor, business owner in his social circle suddenly began digging into his history of giving. They found out that he also started an incubator program with his own funds to help fledgling entrepreneurs. From then, it was on.

Tony got an increasing amount of invitations, and at first, he had no problem accepting some of them. Then, people started asking him to read their business plans, listen to pitches for ideas for businesses, and one bold person even asked him to finance his project! And yes, you guessed it. Those simple invitations out for coffee and lunch turned into a nightmare for Tony. Now because everyone was becoming aware of the good deeds he had done, other people wanted to benefit as well. The very thing he was trying to avoid was now the biggest thorn in his side. How was he to know what would happen as a result of that damned news story?

Tony knew he had to put a stop to it because he couldn't possibly help everyone. He just wanted to keep his friendships and go back to an unassuming life. So he tried telling people to not discuss business matters during social time. Some people got offended and labeled him as uncooperative and stuck up. Yes, Tony, the fun guy everyone wanted to hang out with. Because he decided to draw a clear line between party time and business, he was now being accused of being stuck up. Some people were understanding, but the brain pickers and opportunists weren't so forgiving and they caused a lot of stress for Tony.

I'd like to say Tony was able to put an end to all of the shenanigans and everything went back to normal, but I can't. Tony ended up disassociating himself with a lot of people that he formerly had the pleasure of hanging out with. Those people, relentless in their efforts, kept pushing and pushing and finally he just had enough. Some would argue that maybe he should have been honest up front about who he was and what he did, and a lot of the hoopla could have been avoided. Some would also argue that it wouldn't have harmed anyone if he had met a couple of their demands. But I feel Tony did the right thing.

Some people just don't know how to respect boundaries, and why should you suffer for their poor manners or insensitivity? There is a time and place for everything and people who can't understand that or who push the issue just have to suffer the consequences. Shame on them.

Chapter 5
Hire Me, Not My Idea

How many times have you gone on an interview only to have it turn into an inquisition or an unpaid workday? You go into an interview full of promise, and hopeful that you can wow the interviewer into giving you the job because you're the best candidate. All is going well until the moment when the interviewer asks you to map out a strategy, soup to nuts, for a project. You know, just so that *he* knows that you know your stuff. I mean after all, you are this extraordinarily talented individual and in order for him to really know this, he needs to do his best to get you to spill everything you know. Just for proof and *his* peace of mind, right?

Then, you get that deer in a headlights look. You start to panic because you don't know what to do. You want to make sure you stand out above the other candidates, but inside your gut, you feel there should be boundaries. Your heart and your head are in conflict because you don't know how to draw those boundaries without hurting feelings or risking losing out on a potentially great job…or are you?

On the one hand, you want to make a great impression. You want to make sure they know what they will get if they choose to hire you instead of the other guy. You want to show your stuff and prove that you are a valuable asset to the team and the company. You want to show that you can come in the gate with great ideas and an action plan to make improvements from day one in the job. On the other hand, if you give up all of this information *on the first date*, you risk being replaceable. They could very well just be looking for a quick fix and have no intention of hiring you or anyone else for that matter. If you spill it all, then why would they need you? It's a tough situation to be in.

Because I'm a recruiter, I sit on both sides of the fence when it comes to interviews. It is my job to get as much information about a person and their abilities as I can in the sixty to ninety minutes I spend with them in a formal interview. This is the time I dig in deep to get a better understanding of what makes the candidate tick and how they could fit in and be an asset to the company. I have to know that you are the top choice and that you have the know-how, the fit and the capacity to do the job as well as fit in with the team. Sometimes an in depth situational interview (where I give scenarios and gauge a candidate's responses and effectiveness) is a way for me to determine if you can apply your skills, knowledge and accomplishments from the past to what you could do in the future with my client.

I understand from the candidate side that you have to be guarded with what you share. When you have a special set of skills, it's human nature to want to brag on them or showcase them in some way so people take notice and respect you for your talents. But at times, you must be guarded and rightly so. In a tough economy such as the one we're in now, companies are notorious for trying to pick people's brains so they can pull together a hodgepodge of solutions into a strategy for themselves so they don't have to make a hire. It's not just limited to consultants either. Many job categories that utilize knowledge are prime targets for brain picking.

Let's take Social Media Managers for instance. Although it's been around in some capacity during the last decade, social media is still considered in its infancy. While many social media agencies will say that they can apply metrics to measure the probability of success, this simply isn't true. Social media is dependent on a number of things and the most important is how your team or manager implements the strategy and how receptive the audience is. Brands vary just as people vary, so what may work for my company may or may not work for the next. It is therefore an intangible service. People who were early adopters before the introduction of courses and certifications by schools learned from the ground up. But it doesn't diminish or lessen their knowledge or effectiveness. Still, some companies, because they themselves don't know how to measure it, are not convinced that anyone without a degree or certification can be successful.

Now we find ourselves at a stalemate. People with experience in social media are hard pressed to prove their worth and effectiveness. With so many so-called gurus on the market telling people how easy it is to make thousands of dollars a month with a $27 solution, it makes it harder for legitimate social media connoisseurs to be taken serious or even considered worthy of making certain salaries. I know, it sucks, but you can beat this kind of attitude. A hiring manager may not automatically be a sneaky snake trying to get over by picking your brain. He could simply not know how to measure effectively your talents in order to make a sound decision.

The kneejerk reaction is to ask someone to create a hypothetical strategy. To the interviewer, this might be a normal part of the process. But what they don't know is this is an invasion and an insult to some people. In essence, they are asking you to lay everything out on the table so they can make a decision. That's not the smartest way to go, especially with a startup company or one that is not as widely recognized. Granted, some people will let companies like Google x-ray their brain and take their first born just to get a foot in the door (and they know this too!). But once that practice becomes standard with the big boys, you can bet your last dollar word will get around and other companies will adopt the same practice, intentional or otherwise.

So what to do about this growing problem. Well, you can't just skip interviews, and you can't just get angry and storm out. How you react will depend on how you are approached by an interviewer. Let's take a look at two different approaches and I'll lay out strategies for handling both.

In Scenario A we have a company notorious for being cheap. They have a long list of disgruntled consultants who are tired of the hassle of being nickel and dimed by the company. They want the maximum options for the lowest cost and aren't afraid to co-opt an idea or three to keep it moving. They are notorious for bringing in a variety of candidates to interview for a phantom position (yes, those do exist…well, you know what I mean) so they can get a wide range of possible solutions to their problems. They advertise a position or two, carefully craft the job description and set out to find the best candidates to *hire*. They make it so interesting that lots of people apply.

When the interview process begins, they are sure to include a panel for candidates to meet, each lobbing in depth questions and problems (hypothetical of course) and take plenty of notes. You may have seen these panel interviews, probably at the second round once you get past the recruiter. You, the unsuspecting candidate, feel a little under the pressure, but you hold your own. You notice that two out of the five panelists don't seem to be very impressed with your answers. Their facial expressions have really freaked you out. But you stand your ground and give it all you've got.

Then you think *OK, I need a Hail Mary moment*, and you mention a plan you thought of as you were researching the company and preparing for your interview. Bingo. They've got your ass hooked now. As you proceed to lay out in detail, this hypothetical plan, they're taking notes, and planning on discussing after amongst themselves. They thank you for your time and let you know someone will be in touch soon with a decision. But not to worry because *you did great*! Weeks pass, and either the position is on hold, they went with someone else or they decided not to hire at all. Hhhmmm.

Trust me when I say this is not an every day occurrence, but I want you to be on the look out for this kind of foolishness. When you are interviewing for any position, it is important that you always do your research. Social media and the Internet make it almost impossible to NOT do research on a company. Someone somewhere has most likely interviewed with them and can share their experience. I don't think current employees would be willing to share their experiences, but those who didn't make the cut, they are fair game. They are under no obligation to keep their interview process a secret. And if the interview was disastrous in any way, believe they will be sharing it amongst their social network.

You can avoid this kind of brain picking interview by research, as I said above, by going into the interview with confidence, and by learning how to read the signs early on so you can control how the flow of the interview goes. Don't be intimidated by a person's title or the fact that you're meeting with a panel of people. They are just people. If they came to you, obviously they saw something in you that made them feel you might be a fit. Your information, knowledge or skill is what they need. Sure you may need a job, but they need someone to fulfill their needs. Now this isn't free license to get crazy or overly cocky. I'm just giving you the mental leverage you need.

When you encounter a situation such as the one described above, it's important to maintain your cool. Learn to ask great questions because it helps with that mental leverage I just told you about. For instance, when an interviewer wants to know how you would handle a certain issue, ask them if it is something they currently are having problems with and why they think this is the case. Share with them a similar situation and how you were able to successfully navigate the issue. Share the end results (increase in sales, reduced turn around, etc.) as a result of your process or strategy. Then tell them that you can't reveal each step of the process because you owe confidentiality to your former boss.

Now, be prepared, because you will no doubt get push back if you use this with certain interviewers. They are relentless and they want to know specifically how you would solve their problem. I would turn it around on them once again. For example, I've been interviewed about how I would improve diversity at a company. What they wanted was an all out diversity strategy to help them with compliance issues. I asked them to tell me what they've done in the past and what the previous diversity manager had in mind, but wasn't successful in implementing.

When that information was shared, I was able to pull specific examples to share with them. I did not divulge any resources (which is what they wanted) as I was very general in my responses. I invoked the why, what, how rule. Sure I told them why they needed to increase brand awareness in certain communities, and what communities they needed. But I didn't get specific with names of groups or organizations. I showed them the results of my campaigns without giving them all of the intricacies of the campaign. Did it piss them off? A little, perhaps. But it protected me. Stand your ground and protect as much information as you can. That's your leverage and either they want that knowledge or they don't. Just know that you can take control of the flow. If the interview is still heading in an uncomfortable direction, don't be afraid to end it and walk away.

Don't let your ego or the other person's misgivings affect your mood or performance. Never make assumptions about them (jealousy, insecure, afraid I'll take their job) because when you do, you start driving yourself crazy, you'll unintentionally bruise their ego, or you'll find yourself kicked out of the interview. I don't care if they are pulling this brain-picking stunt because of jealousy or whatever. You do not lower yourself to fall for the bait. It's *their* hang-up, not yours. Do not argue or accuse. Keep your mouth shut, hold your head up high, if you're a spiritual person, say a silent prayer for them, then keep it moving.

Let's look at Scenario B. Not everyone is as cunning or ill-willed as the interviewer in the last scenario. In this scenario you have the well-meaning and perhaps unskilled interviewer who is just trying to honestly assess your skills. I've seen these types before. In fact, I've consulted with and trained them in the art of effective interviewing. Nobody has ever taught them how to conduct an interview so they're just winging it. A few of them may even tell you that they're not used to interviewing up front.

During the interview, they start asking you to lay out a plan for them that could be implemented on day one should they hire you. You have to be careful here.

If he is simply unskilled in the interview etiquette, you can employ the same tactic as you did with the other scenario. Start asking questions whose answers will give you insight into the true problem. In order for this to work, you must have done your research. Interviews are not one way. Candidates are allowed to ask questions too. In fact, you'll probably earn more brownie points by showing your interest and they'll see you really want the job. Make sure you relay back to them the problem they are having from your perception and ask them if you understood this to be correct. Now you have some room to work.

More times than not, they just want to know you can do the job and solve their problem. By offering examples of work you've done in the past (and the positive outcomes based upon your involvement and execution) you show them that you have encountered similar issues and know how to manage them. Talk about how they see those examples fitting in with what they need at their company. Ask them based on your history, how they would see you fitting in. And if you have a few solutions in mind, please do not map them out at this point. Instead tell them at the end of the conversation that you've had a chance to run some strategies through your mind during your conversation with them and you can't wait to work with them to make them happen.

This makes them excited about you as a candidate, and shows that should you be the hire, you'll already have the foundations to hit the ground running. Don't lie and tell them you have some things in mind when you really don't. If they hire you and you come in with nothing, they'll feel duped. Then you'll get fired. It is not uncommon to map out strategies or processes in your mind as you're interviewing and getting a clear look at the real nitty gritty. When I take on recruiting clients, I have to do this during our meetings because many times, they don't have a strategy. When I share that I had some things in mind, more times than not, they are curious and can't wait to get started. The same thing can work for you if you really want the job. And you don't have to give up all you know before you get an offer.

Sometimes you'll find yourself in an innocent situation with an inexperienced interviewer. Don't get offended when you're asked to prove your skills. Instead, as I showed you how twice in this chapter, turn the interview around to your favor. Use their pain points to ask questions that give you better insight. Then relate past similar experiences so they know that you get it and can deliver. You should never feel obligated to prove yourself by going above and beyond in an interview. Yes, you want to let them see what you bring to the table, but no, you don't have to give it all away and put yourself at risk of not getting the job. Practice your why, what, how method until you've perfected it. I'm telling you, you'll become better as a candidate and you'll surely impress hiring managers.

Marilyn's Story

Marilyn was out of work for about seven months when she came to me. She was beyond frustrated because she had been on countless interviews, some of them second and third interviews, but hadn't received one offer. She couldn't understand it. Her resume was impeccable, she kept her social media profiles up to date, her reputation (brand) was on fire and she had worked with some of the biggest firms in the industry. When she got laid off from her last job, she figured she would be out of work at the most two months. And truth be told, she didn't really try too hard those first two months. But when her emergency fund started thinning out, she realized it was time to get back to work.

Marilyn was a publicist and the unfortunate victim of downsizing and the economy. The company had to cut back and she was caught up in the second round of layoffs. During her tenure, she kept up on all of the latest trends and requirements in public relations. She even was an early adopter in social media when most of her colleagues dismissed it as a fad. Her efforts landed clients in prime media pieces for print and television. So needless to say she was bankable.

Instead of going out on her own and starting her own firm, Marilyn preferred the steady weekly paycheck. She did some freelance work on occasion, but for the most part she had no interest in starting or running a business. So this meant she had to go to work. But, nobody was hiring, or at least, not hiring *her*. At first she thought it was because she had such a heavy emphasis on social media. She made sure she was clear in her resume and in her interviews that she was a well-rounded public relations specialist. She had samples of work she had done, media clips from her clients, and she wrote a blog that was very popular within the PR community. People loved her and they loved her no holds barred advice.

Marilyn noticed that each time she went on an interview, specifically with smaller or newer firms, she left the interview process feeling like she had just been interrogated. She was 25, bright, and it was obvious she had a bright future in PR with the right company. On one occasion, she interviewed with the recruiter and the hiring manager and they loved her. They thought she had fresh perspectives and would fit in great with the team. She had to go on one final interview with the vice president of the company. The moment Marilyn walked through the door, she could feel the tension. Immediately from the first hello, the vice president did not seem to like her. She didn't like this because every liked her, well usually.

No matter how Marilyn answered this lady's question, there was a counter. No matter how much she showed her expertise (which actually dated back to senior year in high school, all through college and well into her career) this lady found a way to throw it back at her as if to say she was unimpressive and wasting her time. Needless to say, the interview did not go well and she didn't get the job.

The next interview was strange. This time Marilyn met directly with the hiring manager. He was the decision maker so there would be no other person to speak to. She had one shot to make an impression and after that last interview, she was surely going to do better. This company, an interactive digital media company, was relatively new. It had been in business for a year and a half, but they were already making a name for themselves. Their reputation was phenomenal. So Marilyn was pleased when she got a call for the interview.

Things started off very well. The hiring manager seemed impressed with her as they chit chatted about their respective views on PR and social media. He was impressed with her wealth of knowledge and kept remarking that she'd make an excellent addition to the team, but without implying she had the job. Then just as the conversation was getting comfortable, things took a sharp turn when the hiring manager told her they were having a problem with three accounts. He asked her to tell him what she would do to turn it around. But here's the catch. He wanted her to take the problems home and work on them for 48 hours, then come back in the office with a game plan. At that moment, big blazing alarms went off in her head and she knew something was off. However, she agreed and left the office.

On her way home she thought about it and the more she thought, the less comfortable she was. After all, there was no offer on the table and these were their real clients. Why on earth should she do work that she wasn't getting paid for? Was this a test? Did he want to see if she could handle the accounts? Did he want to see if she could even come up with strategies? Would he hire her if she got it right? Marilyn had a lot of questions and a lot of doubts.

The next day, she sent him an email telling him that she felt uncomfortable mapping out three entire strategies. If he were a client, he would have to pay a retainer up front. (See, and she didn't think she had what it took to be an entrepreneur). He responded that if she wanted the job, he had to make sure she knew her stuff. He assured her it was common practice and couldn't wait to see what she came up with. It was quite dismissive if you ask me. So Marilyn met with some friends and posed the scenario to them. Immediately two of the three said not to do it. He was just using her to work out his problems and probably wouldn't hire her. The third insisted that if she needed to jump through hoops to get a paycheck in this economy, she'd lend her the tutu.

Marilyn stood her ground. While she needed a job, she wasn't willing to sacrifice herself to get it. Her brand, her knowledge, her skills have all earned her a stellar reputation. She called (yes on the phone) and told the hiring manager that she appreciated his time, but she couldn't do work that she wouldn't be compensated for. While a bit perplexed, he did tell her he understood. The company went on to hire an outside consultant to create a strategy but then got rid of her to tweak it and use it as their own. Marilyn dodged a big bullet with that company.

In the end, Marilyn realized that she is not the problem. But she also realized that she needed to get clarity on how to handle situations like these and figure out her strength. She knew what she brought to the table and had to make others respect it. She no longer wastes her time and she is very careful about how much information she will divulge during an interview. She gives them just enough to see what she has accomplished in the past, and how it makes her a top pick as a candidate today. I'm happy to report that Marilyn did find work as a contractor. While the work is temporary, it allows her to network with the right people and get her brand out there in a big way. She is no longer cheating herself or trying to give away the cow with the milk just to prove she can do a job.

Chapter 6
The Barter Experience-
Like Begets Like

Aside from volunteer or philanthropic work, there are times when I will do work for someone without charging them actual dollars. This is called **Bartering**. Bartering (or alternative trade, reciprocal capital, etc.) is exchanging services between two individuals or businesses for equal or in-kind value (like value for like value). When someone wants to pick your brain and they have something you want or will want, consider bartering for it. A good majority of people will be open to the idea of bartering with you if you have something they feel is worth exchanging. When you agree to barter, be sure it is **mutually** beneficial. If, for example, you are asked to write a press release by an attorney, you can't expect them to give you a month of free legal advice in exchange. That's not a balanced trade.

But you will also find some who will not be open to it. For whatever reason, bartering still doesn't resonate with a lot of people. In my opinion, I think it's because they don't understand the etiquette or the logistics of it. I have a friend, Allison, who started her business on a shoestring and made bartering the life's blood of her business. She isn't the type to pick people's brains without wanting to pay them in some regard. I'll get more into her story later in this chapter.

Bartering for services puts you in an advantageous bargaining position because you both stand to gain something of value without having to invest real money. If someone requests free information or help, you must feel comfortable in asking for an in kind value service in exchange. This is not a time to be shy, especially if you know the person is not in a position to pay you in dollars. Assess what they have that can be of benefit to you that will offset the cost of helping them out. If they are genuine, they should have no problem in an even exchange of knowledge. Only you will know if what they have is equal to what you're giving. So don't be afraid to bring up bartering as an option.

So how do you determine if bartering is ideal for your situation? That's easy. First, you assess the situation by asking yourself a few questions.

Why is this person coming to you? If this is a person genuinely in need and open to working something out with you in exchange for helping, then you may have a qualified bartering partner. You'll usually find out if a person is willing to barter when you get to the last question on that list I mentioned when I talked about qualifying people a few chapters back. When you ask them about setting up a consultation, and they say they don't have a budget to move forward at this time, but perhaps in the future, do a mental inventory of the potential services they can offer you.

What do they have that I am interested in? Perhaps they're really good at marketing, or they write killer copy. Or maybe they are a fantastic designer, or maybe they're great at styling people. The service doesn't have to be directly related to their business. I once had a young lady who was a makeup artist but she was heavily connected in the media. We bartered me coaching her to grow her makeup artist business and she introduced me to some key media contacts, which led me to some great exposure and a speaking gig. So be open to the obvious and not so obvious potential tradeoffs. And make sure they would be willing to trade said service!

What is the value of their services as compared to

mine? In order for bartering to work, you both have to feel like you've gotten equal value. I can't set up someone's recruiting team and only get a one-hour massage in return. That's not fair and equal. We're talking tens of thousands of dollars on my end, compared to what, maybe $200? No dice. So do an inventory of each service you might be interested in and compare to what they're asking of you. This is a great time to pull out those fee schedules and use them as guides. And if you find yourself still coming up short, think past existing services and look at the not so obvious ones.

Put everything in writing. That is the number one rule in business (next to make a profit). If you are trusting enough to work on a handshake and the other person bails out, you're left with nothing to protect you. Most formal bartering programs have their members sign an agreement form and sign off on a code of conduct or ethics. A couple of organizations that come to mind are: International Reciprocal Trade Association (IRTA)- www.irta.com; International Monetary Systems (IMS)- www.imsbarter.com; National Association of Trade Exchanges (NATE)- www.natebarter.com and The Gigafree Network- www.gigafree.com/barter.html. Please note, inclusion of these organizations does not constitute an endorsement by me or Empower Me! Corporation. There are also many bartering groups, formal and informal, online and in your local area. Just do an Internet search on barter, bartering groups, exchange groups and trade groups. You can even find groups on social media sites such as Facebook, Linked In and Google+. And ask your local Chamber of Commerce for recommendations.

If you find yourself in a situation where the other person

has nothing of value to exchange with you, ask them for a *paying referral*. There is nothing wrong with this, especially if they are very well connected and are in a position to make introductions. I know it can feel strange or even intrusive to ask something like this, but if they are not in a position to pay you, and have nothing of value (for you) to bargain with, this is the next best thing.

If they truly want your expertise, they have to be willing to help you out too. It's kind of like the Equal Exchange point I made above mashed up with paying it forward. Before you dispense any advice, ask them to provide you with referrals to others who most certainly need (and can afford) your service. Figure out who they know that you need to know, and make a list. Ask for the introduction as a condition of helping them out.

Most people are on the level and you shouldn't have to worry about them jerking you around or stalling you on introductions. But every now and then, you have that one person who either doesn't really have connections (they just talk a good, fast game and name drop) or they are super secretive about who they know for fear that someone will come in and usurp their place in the *clique*. I find these types quite comical. So comical, it's pathetic, but I digress.

If you run into this type of person, I wouldn't give any advice or help without at least one important introduction. You can give it to them in doses. The more introductions (that get you in the door), the more help you give. I've been called selfish for this tactic but you know what? It works. You're actually building a trust between you and it shows that you are a person of your word, as is the other person.

You can't barter what you don't have. So don't get in the

habit of over promising and under delivering to people. Not only will you burn bridges, you will also prove yourself to be untrustworthy. It's not always just about what the other person can do for you. You have to safeguard your reputation as well. As big as the business community is, it can be very tiny. People talk and share their experiences, especially the bad ones. So make sure you treat each prospective bartering partner with five star respect.

Make sure when you barter, it makes sense. I know I mentioned above that you should look out for services that compliment each other when considering bartering partnerships. Examples of logical bartering trades include an author with a new book coming out with a huge following offering to do a guest blog post on a site that needs more traffic, bringing their following and giving the blogger a whole new audience of readers. A publicist starting her own firm who doesn't know much about running a business, who exchanges free PR with a management consultant who specializes in growing startup companies. A salon owner looking to build her brand through speaking who takes on a speaker who needs to get and maintain a new look so she can get exposed to speaking opportunities. I can go on, but hopefully you get the point.

Bartering can be a fantastic business strategy, especially when you are lucky enough to find a complimentary match. You can barter with different people for different reasons at any time. Make it a point to always be proactive about building a list of potential bartering partners. It may be a one time or a recurring arrangement. But don't overlook it. And it can be a great leveraging tool for those who constantly encounter brain pickers.

Allison's Story

Allison is a brand new business owner. She decided to go on her own after being disappointed in her job search efforts, and the market itself. She took a leap of faith and decided to start an education company. She already had inside help from her husband, who was a web developer. The Internet is the great playing field leveler, so logistically she could get started building her brand and her company with minimal investment. Her husband build an incredible website based on her specifications, and they got her social media presence established. She was on her way.

Allison had many great ideas about her company, but kept finding herself coming up short in a lot of areas, especially in her finances. Because she was the typical bootstrapping entrepreneur, any cash that came in went right back into the company, leaving little room to do anything else. Allison became frustrated when she had to pass up on more than a few opportunities to grow her brand because she simply didn't have the money to pursue them. So she sat down and started thinking of ways to bring in additional income.

The problem was, every new idea would require her to put in more hours than she had available, and would have taken her away from the true purpose of her business. One day a friend mentioned bartering to Allison. She decided to investigate further and found out there were two local bartering groups right in her city. She contacted them for more information, and was invited to attend the next meeting. Having never bartered before, she didn't know what to expect. At first she had thoughts of other struggling business owners trying to trade things she had no use for. But she quickly decided she would reserve judgment until the meeting.

At the first group's meeting, Allison got to know the key players. She quickly learned that this was a serious group of businesswomen who were all about business. The group was a nurturing learning environment where members came not only to barter, but to make business happen. And one of the things she loved most was that it didn't matter what you had to barter with, there was someone that needed what you had. They had a pay it forward kind of atmosphere as well. If you had a need for someone's service, but they didn't need yours, you could opt to give your service to someone else, as long as they were part of the group.

In other words, if Mary is a social media strategist who needs web design service, and Barbara does web design but doesn't need social media help but needs to learn how to market, and Allison needs social media help and can provide marketing training, then Mary can get web design from Barbara, Barbara can get marketing training from Allison, and Allison can get social media help from Mary. And all of this still falls within the confines of the bartering group rules. Sounds confusing, doesn't it? But not really. Someone is always benefitting and nobody is being left out.

Allison loved this group and was able to get several very important services to help grow her business, and at the same time, was building brand awareness and helping others as well.

The second group didn't turn out so well. They didn't have an open, pay it forward bartering system like the first group did. They had a database and a monthly meeting that was mandatory for all members. She never found anyone to barter with. Nobody ever offered a service she could use, with the exception of bookkeeping services, and nobody was ever interested in any training services from her. The policies were too restrictive and the group didn't yield the desired results.

Allison took her bartering experience beyond her bartering group. By joining the first group, she built the confidence to use bartering as a strategic tool to grow her business. She consistently has people coming to her to develop a training program or to pick her brain (or brainstorm...as they like to call it) to come up with their own creative training programs without wanting or having to pay Allison. She took the principles she learned from her group and applied them on a case-by-case basis. Over time, she has built an impressive network and she no longer finds herself being subjected to brain picking expeditions. And rarely does anyone get offended or put off by her approach of suggesting bartering. Remember, teach a man to fish...

When they can't pay you, consider bartering. The worst that could happen is they say no or don't have anything of value to trade. The best that could happen is you end up helping one another and it's a win-win for all.

Chapter 7
Freebies, Get Your Freebies!

OK, so exactly when is it acceptable to give away freebies to people? That depends on your goals, your business and your heart. I only allow freebies in limited situations and certain people. Bartering and philanthropic work has already been covered. I just want to go over a few other instances where you should allow freebies to brain pickers and how to neutralize them so they don't become a time drain or a habit.

If you are anything like me, you have built your brand by writing, broadcasting, appearing in the media, networking, volunteering and sharing on social media. Don't forget hard work and perfecting your craft. As I mentioned earlier, I have a newsletter, a radio show, a blog, I write for different sites, have been in the media and I'm all over social networking sites dispensing advice. So I have no qualms about telling someone, especially if they are relentless in their pursuit of my brain, to check out any of my freely available resources.

Don't be afraid to refer them to your already existing free resources you have made available online. If you already have archived content on the web in which you dispense advice, refer them to that information and keep it moving. Explain that it's the **only** free information you offer. They should be able to have their basic questions answered by looking up that content.

Make it easy for them to find it by ensuring you have optimized the content and have easy links from your website, social media profiles and even in your email signatures. Anything specific or beyond what's readily available has a cost and they need to know and understand this. Make sure you tell them this. Sometimes if you are very detailed in your free resources, they will be content with checking them out and they'll leave you alone. But if your available information is vague or general in nature, be prepared for them to keep trying to come back with more questions. So make sure that you are meticulous with your content to answer the basic questions.

You can also create a FAQs (or Frequently Asked Questions) page. While FAQ pages could be considered dated by some, people still use them. But don't just use the FAQs to answer the top asked questions. Also use it to explain your policies and why you charge. Could this be considered crass? Yes, but who cares. If you're not yet comfortable telling people there is a charge for certain information, this will do the trick. But I caution you against using it as a substitute for telling them yourself. Some of you might try to hide behind a FAQ page, but you're only delaying the inevitable. You will eventually have to have those conversations about charging, so you may as well start practicing.

The next freebie you may give away to brain pickers is the free consultation. Lots of service providers and consultants will offer potential clients a free consultation with the hopes that it will convert them into paying clients. In theory, this is a great idea. You get to know the client, they get to have a little taste of what you do, and you mutually decide whether or not to work together. It's a vetting process for both sides. While I do occasionally give free consultations, and I think they are great for *some* professionals, I'm not 100% sold on them for everyone.

The sad reality is that free consultations rarely convert to paying clients. If the person is a serious brain picker, then they're going to try to leverage that free consultation into a quick fix for their business or problem. They're not looking to move forward beyond only what they need. From their perspective, they hear the word "consultation" and wrongly assume that it means something bigger than it is. Remember when I said the word *consultation* should change the way you engage a brain picker? Well it does...if they understand the *concept* of a consultation and you know how and when to draw the line.

When business owners or professionals are starting out, the first thing they're looking for are ways to grow business. They want to attract as many clients as possible to keep their practice going. There is nothing wrong with that. But as with anything, you have to take the good with the bad. And when offering anything for free, there's a good chance things will go well, but a greater chance that it will go bad. It's good to believe that people's motives are pure, but recognize that some are not.

Remember a few chapters back when I talked about Donna, and how she started giving away free time and information to build brand awareness? It backfired on her, didn't it? She was so focused on gaining popularity and acknowledgement of her skills that she didn't think things through. She thought nothing of giving free consults out to anyone who asked. The problem was she kept getting her brain picked with zero conversion. Had Donna leveraged those consultations into an opportunity to hook her prospects into wanting more, had she given them an opportunity to get a peek at what results she could accomplish for them, she might have had a higher conversion rate. Instead, she left the ball in their court by not having a strong call to action nor did she properly follow up to close the deals.

If you agree to give free consultations, be prepared to

have to accept a lower conversion rate unless you make it so they want more (and are not afraid to pay for it). Consultations, if done correctly, can be used to educate your brain picker on what you do and convince them to trust you to move forward in the process. Under normal circumstances, this does work to convert some new clients. But for the brain picker, you'll find yourself jumping through a lot of hoops just to prove yourself to them. And still, they won't buy from you.

I know some sales professionals out there will complain *well that's because they're doing it wrong. Anyone can be converted to a paying client.* I beg to differ. Brain pickers aren't like real clients. They're like those coupon ladies you see on television. They're on a mission to get the most for the least and are not ashamed, intimidated or impressed by some fancy sales process. They're not meant to be sold to.

A free consultation is supposed to be a chance for you to change their minds. This is where that *why, what, how* rule comes into play. Make sure you're asking the right questions to get to the heart of their problem. Use those answers to illustrate how you've helped similar clients in the past. Drive home the point that your past clients were once just like them, and they were able to see results or overcome whatever issue they had with your help. Appeal to their desire to improve. Remember, they can be tough nuts to crack because they're not looking to spend money.

If you insist that free consultations are essential for your business, try doing it in a different way. Many traditional consults are one-to-one, where you are investing lots of time with many *individuals* and losing out on billable hours. Try the one-to-many consultation. Now, technically it can't be called a consultation because you are not spending time with each individual and their concern. If you gather a group of people with the same or similar issues or questions, you can create a workshop or call (I really don't care for teleconferences) that will speak to that one specific issue or several and give them an opportunity to become a client afterwards. That way you will leverage your time and can simultaneously reach a broad number of people.

But hold on. This isn't an excuse for you to get slimy with it and *push message* or worse, *bait and switch*. There are plenty of people who hold these calls and workshops with the intention of not to educate, but to sell their garbage. It turns into a pitch fest where the facilitator keeps talking about their product or service more than actually giving information as advertised. As a true professional, I would hope that you would be on the level and make this a truly educational experience. Remember, this call or workshop should be educational not an ambush.

There nothing I hate more than signing up for what's supposed to be an information session, that turns into a brag session on how rich and successful a person is and how if I want to be rich too, I will buy their course/coaching/mastermind bullshit. That's not authentic. You can educate people and still end up making sales or closing clients from these workshops and calls. If you educate people and give them just enough of the information they need to be impressed and see how it could benefit them by working with you, they will want more. If you're worried about how you will be received, just speak from the insights and expertise gained from your own life experiences. Come from a place of honesty and sincerity. Be sure to give a well-organized and well-presented call or workshop that helps people and answers their *basic* questions. If you've done that, and done your best, people will want to become clients.

Keep in mind though, while you may get a high number of initial signups for the free session, you won't sign all of them as paying clients. Remember, brain pickers are not meant to be sold to. But you can use this as a vetting process to weed out the real clients from the brain pickers. I hate to say it, but in my experience, when you offer anything for free, you will attract a large percentage of people who will **never, ever** buy from you no matter what you do (or can do) for them. That's just not what they're there for and you shouldn't feel bad about it. So don't internalize it.

I'm not saying don't ever offer free stuff, quite the contrary. Just be prepared to get a lower conversion rate with certain crowds. Offering things (like the call or workshop) that are low cost for you to deliver and high perceived value to them keeps you from wasting your time. Things that take your time on a one-to-one basis have a HIGH cost (your time) to deliver. It is time that you can't sell to anyone else, get back, and time you could be spending on other projects (with PAYING clients). So why should you invest that much of your time on non-prospects? But this isn't a sales lesson so let's move on.

Another way to give freebies is to select people to **gift** your services to. This does fall under philanthropic work but I want to expound upon it. When you decide to gift services to people, do it on your own terms. As in the case of Tony a few chapters back, you might want to make it a habit of keeping it quiet that you do this. The last thing you want is for people to know you do this because then they will hound you. Some may truly need it, but many will be trying to game the system to get what they want and use you to get it. I know, I sound cynical. But I've been around a long time and it's human economics to want more for less. And I've seen it myself firsthand.

The way I choose people to gift my services to is by watching on social media and through networking with people. When you get to know people, you get a look into their struggles as well. I pay attention to discussions and forums and try to follow people that capture my interest. It's not just about them posting or talking about their challenges. It's about watching how they share with others, how they reach out to help others even if they may not have all the answers themselves, and whether or not they channel their frustrations for good or selfish purposes.

In other words, I don't gift my services to people who spend their time on social media (or in person) complaining about what they don't have, who's holding them back, and why they can never get ahead. There's something to be said for humility.

I know in advance when I'll be having an event or launching a service that could benefit others. Sometimes I may be beta testing something and need to select impartial people to really give it a test run and give me honest feedback so I can adjust accordingly. Is this a bit selfish? Perhaps. But I still get to give back and it's a win-win for us all and I make no apologies for that.

Choose wisely before you give. While I do a lot of observing before I make my decisions, I still will run into some people who are unappreciative. Hell, I even run into people who after all of that **still** want more from me! People will get away with what you let them get away with. So as with everything else

I've said in this book, do your due diligence and trust your gut.

The only *payment* requirement I have of people to whom I gift my services is that they give a real testimonial on the results of working with me. This is a small price to pay especially if you've just given them thousands of dollars of services that they otherwise wouldn't have been able to afford that has helped them improve or solve a problem. I haven't had anyone say no yet, but I have had a few who said they would then didn't. I don't get angry about stuff like this. Even when you are doing the giving with no expectations in return, some people will still take advantage. It's a chance you must take. Make sure you get testimonials in exchange for your gift.

When bearing free gifts, sometimes people can be a bit skeptical, especially if they don't really know you too well. Or, they may be weary of strings attached to a gift. So the defenses may go up. Unfortunately, it's a sign of the times so don't take offense to it. If someone wants to doubt your credibility, before you react, first try to understand where their apprehension comes from. Talk with them to get insight on why they feel this way and answer any questions they have so you can ease their minds. Don't take offense because you know their just trying to protect themselves. Provide them with as much information as you can to help them decide if they want to move forward. Use information available about yourself on the web to emphasize the point of why you are the ideal person to work with. Don't invest too much time or energy trying to convince them though. Remember, we all want clients, but don't waste time on dead leads. Keep it moving.

If they are just ignorant about it, meaning they're being

purposely cynical just for the hell of it, then by all means point them to the Internet to figure it out. No need to waste your time trying to prove anything to them, because they really only want to get what they can from you for free and will purposely make it difficult. There's nothing to see there so keep moving right along and don't look back. And don't feel guilty about it either. You didn't lose out on anything.

Dan's Story

Dan was an accountant who wanted to switch gears in his life and career. He spent the last fifteen years as an accountant for a major firm and was ready to move on to something more stimulating. Sure, he was great at numbers. He was the numbers guy and everyone counted (no pun intended) on him. But Dan wanted to move into teaching. He was sure he didn't want to teach at a college, but he felt that he could best serve people by teaching small businesses how to set up effective accounting for their companies.

He didn't want to take on small businesses as accounting clients. He had no desire to do the actual accounting work any more. Nor did he want to run an accounting practice on his own. Dan had seen so many of his friends, small business owners, make huge mistakes in their accounting practices. So he felt that his knowledge and expertise would help companies like these create better accounting practices for themselves.

Dan had saved up enough money to leave his job and go out on his own. He had put aside enough money to manage his expenses (personal and business) for at least a year. He planned everything down to the last details and would be working from a home office to save money. But his main problem was how would he get clients? It's hard enough trying to win accounting business, since most times companies were either doing it in house or were loyal to their current accountants. Trying to convince them to let him create a training program was a harder sell because they needed *accounting* not *training*.

Dan had heard of these free calls that people did called teleclasses. With minimal investment (just paying for enough lines to accommodate the call) you can host a call, have people dial in to listen, and make an audio available later. He thought this was a great idea. He could get a couple of classes going, but charge a fee, and make it so the recordings were available for replay for thirty days. Simple enough, right? So off he went to plan.

He had a friend create a great postcard and matching email piece that he could send out. He spent two weeks creating the content and when he was ready, he set out on his campaign to market it. He hand delivered postcards to a carefully crafted list of potential clients. He told everyone he knew and asked friends to pass out cards and spread the word. He started sending out email to his mailing list. Then he sat back and waited for registrations to begin.

I won't go into the details of the teleclass, but I do want to focus on what happened when Dan reached out to a supposed friend to help spread the word. This friend had her own business and had dabbled in quite a few things, not really finding success in any one thing. He asked her if she would share the news about his new class, just as he had done with other friends. The friend asked him what it was about and he gave her a little background about the class, and mentioned how people had really been rallying behind him to get the word out.

Well, this *friend*, who was struggling in her own business, was curious about these classes. She wanted him to go into more specific details about how he was conducting the class and what content he'd be teaching. Dan immediately got a bad feeling. He told her the information was proprietary and that she could find out information about the actual teleconferencing services and concept online. He even gave her the links to check out on her own. The friend, frustrated that he wouldn't share specifics, told him she couldn't in *good conscience* promote a class she had never taken. To add insult to injury, she asked him to give her free access to the class so she could "audit it", then she could give a fair review of the class to her network.

Dan was stunned. He never asked her to endorse or review the class. All he wanted her to do was help a friend by spreading the word that he was teaching the class, not be a spokesperson for it. Upset, he asked her what taking the class had to do with telling people about it. She replied that she had a reputation to maintain and if she recommended junk, her reputation would be hurt. But it was funny, because every time in the past when she asked him to share something with his network, he did it no questions asked. Now all of a sudden, she wanted to act in *good conscience*.

Dan finally figured out that this friend was upset that he wouldn't share his information with her so that she could *model* it for her own use. He politely recommended she Google the information she needed and he disassociated himself from her. In the end, she tried to create her own classes, but they failed miserably. Had she not been so underhanded about it, Dan would have helped her out. But, you reap what you sow. Other people's insecurities and ulterior motives are not your problem or your business. Let them work it out.

Dan's teleclass was a hit and lead him to new clients, speaking engagements and two joint venture opportunities.

Chapter 8
Just Google® It & Leave Me Alone!

L et's get into the heart of why people want to suck all of the information from your brain. Wow, that sounds kind of vampirish, doesn't it? But let's be real about what it is. It's not always because they are selfish or don't value other people's intellect. Because information is so readily available and because there are so many charlatans passing themselves off as *gurus* and *experts*, people want to be sure they're getting the real deal. I don't blame them because it's almost like a defense mechanism. They're trying to protect themselves from getting taken. But in trying to protect themselves, they can often cross the line.

I don't fault them in the least bit. It's no fun being taken. And as the economy worsens, and the Internet makes it easier for anyone to throw up a business shingle and call themselves an expert, the amount of scams being reported is on the rise. Actually, there are record numbers being reported. In their quest to make sure a person is on the up and up, people can sometimes overstep boundaries. For some people, getting a consultant or expert to layout a complete strategy or solution may be proof of competency and legitimacy for their own peace of mind.

But for the consultant or expert, it's an insulting and over-reaching imposition. To put it in perspective, it's kind of like going into a grocery store and saying *hey let me drink this carton of milk first just to make sure it's OK and then I'll pay you.* A grocer will throw you out if the store if you try to pull that. But paranoia is real. Is this your fault? No, especially if you're one of the good guys.

Unfortunately we are punished for the sins of others. It comes with the territory and as a professional, you must know how to clearly articulate your value and come up with your own methods to put people's minds at ease from the very beginning. If you've done your job in building your brand, you should have a digital footprint as well as a solid network of people who can vouch for you. You will also have had an impressive track record with clients who will readily sing your praises. And all of this should be documented and freely available.

Don't be afraid to send them to Google you. It's digital and social proof of your abilities freely available on the web. Now hold on a second. If you've read my blog, you would have seen my blog post on how it irritates me to have someone tell me to just *Google them* when I ask for information. Not only do I think it's tacky as hell, but it also makes me think you can't articulate your value to me, and that you really don't have an established brand, just a bunch of stuff on the web. But that's not what I'm talking about here. There is a difference, believe me.

What I'm referring to is building a case for them to work with and trust you, enhanced by the information they can find readily available about you on the Internet. Make sense?

The first thing someone does when they are introduced to or stumbles upon you is check you out on the Internet. With social media and search engines, you can research businesses **and** individuals. Like it or not, whatever information you (or others) put out there about yourself is free for the world to see. Good, bad or indifferent, once you have that footprint out there, people are going to check it out. The more positive the information, the better it is for you. So you should make sure that all of the good stuff is there and coming up first in the search results. I won't get into an optimization lesson here. Just make sure you're being careful with your brand.

Make it easy for people to learn about you by ensuring there is an easy trail to follow. Make sure everything links back to your own site. This includes social media profiles, interviews, write-ups, your own writing, etc. Any time someone mentions you (in a positive way of course) be sure to include a link to it on your site. The more respected external brands, companies and people that mention you and your work, the better it is for you. This should give brain pickers a frame of reference to know what they are dealing with. In addition to a consult, references and samples of your work, this should show them the professional you are and squash any misgivings they may have of you. And if done correctly, deter them from believing they can take advantage of you.

Once again, if you run into a determined brain picker, none of the above will matter. It's not for you to get frustrated or offended by it because remember, some people are just out to get what they can. In situations like this, where even after vetting you, they still want to pick your brain, gladly refer them to the Internet. But not to find your own work. This is where you tell them to (for lack of a better term) kick rocks and go find someone else to harass…but in a nice, professional way.

You can absolutely recommend they go to Google, or any other search engine or to sites that have articles or information about what they need advice on. Let them go pick someone else's brain. If you feel funny about casting them off or sending them away, no worries. You can also recommend books or magazines that might be helpful to them.

Let them expend that energy they would have used in meeting you at Starbucks and hit the search engines to find their answers. They'll be so overwhelmed with the various amounts of information, that it will frustrate them. Not fun for them, but hey, when they're ready to put it in proper perspective and implement, they can come to you...for a consult...a paid consult. My philosophy is it's either them or me (expending energy and valuable time). I'd rather it be them.

I like to do this to the egotistical brain pickers who feel the need to inform me that they can really find the information anywhere and don't really need me. I had one person tell me that I should be *flattered* that he came to me. He said he could always look up the information on his own. Well I told him be my guest, have at it. I don't have time to entertain foolishness.

People will always challenge the authenticity of your knowledge. Sometimes it's warranted, sometimes it's ignorance. But it should never define you or make you feel inadequate. And you definitely shouldn't be jumping through hoops like a circus pony to prove anything to anyone. Everything isn't for everyone, and that's OK. You can't force someone to respect your credibility. You could appear on every major television talk show, have write-ups in all of the major magazines, and speak at all of the major conferences in your industry. There will always be a cynic or three who will work your nerves.

Remember, the cynics aren't your clients. It is not your job to convince them to work with you. If you let them, they will pick at you until you lay out a detailed roadmap for them to follow. And even then, they'll still not be satisfied. Cut your losses and leave them alone. Focus your time and energy on people who truly want or need your help.

Melissa's Story

Melissa is a healthy living expert and certified raw food chef. She is professionally trained in raw food preparation and she is certified to train raw food chefs. During the last eleven years, she has put in a lot of time, money and energy into learning her craft and staying current on the industry, trends and regulations. As her brand grew, she felt it was important to get her message in front of a wider audience. She had done a great job of growing her exclusive list of local clients who were wowed by her service, knowledge and her food. But she wanted to reach more people. Healthy living is such an important topic.

Melissa decided to turn to social media to get her brand out in a bigger and faster way. She did what all the experts recommended and got on Twitter, Facebook, and Linked In. She started a blog and even wrote a newsletter featuring daily tips. Each day she shared information about nutrition, healthy eating, and recipes. All of the experts said that the more you share, the more you draw people into your brand. Melissa was diligent about sharing her information and keeping a constant social media schedule so she could keep her growing audience engaged and informed for better living and healthy eating.

She noticed that her list and following grew exponentially and people were recommending her as a person to follow. She started getting email from people asking for recommendations for preparing certain foods, meal planning and detox aids. She had been sharing tons of content freely and thought it was more than enough. She directed them to her website for more information, but people would continue to ask her. Meanwhile, Melissa was creating programs, writing books and developing recipes to sell in addition to the training and the food preparation services so she could bring in additional revenue streams. After months of planning, testing and writing, she was finally ready to put her products on the market.

Melissa sent out an announcement on her mailing list, posted to Facebook and Twitter and wrote a blog post about her new offerings. She also did a few interviews with radio shows and a few blog sites. It drove tons of new visitors to her website and increased her following. But strangely enough, no orders came in. Frustrated, she decided to revisit her marketing strategy. She had done everything by the book so she was puzzled as to why nobody had signed up for any of the paid services. Then she thought perhaps people weren't clear on what she was offering. So Melissa created a teleclass so that she could talk about the benefits of going raw and introduce her new products and services.

When she announced the free call, 217 people signed up to dial in. Melissa was excited and thought of all the new business she would bring in. Had she finally figured out the right formula? Perhaps. We'll see after the call.

The day came and Melissa held her call. She had a great handout, a fresh blog post and was ready to answer questions of the callers. It was the most informative 90-minute session. She announced that she would be offering a free 32 page e-book to all of the attendees. She also offered a 50% discount for her detox program and a coupon for 25% off any of her services. They ate it up! All 217 people downloaded the e-book and the coupon.

A few weeks later, still nobody signed up or used their coupons. Melissa was perplexed. She had given away a book. She held a call. She continued to share content via her newsletter, blog and social media tools. People seemed very interested and she marketed it to what she thought were the right people. So what the heck went wrong? She couldn't figure it out. Then someone suggested she just come out and ask people why they weren't buying. What she learned was disturbing and eye opening.

Melissa learned that as long as she was giving away so much free content, people didn't feel motivated to pay for anything. She had given it all away for so long, she trained them to expect free information from her. Some bold people even commented that she really didn't share anything earth shattering or new, and that they could find similar information online. These were clearly not her ideal people and she didn't really target the right demographic. Sure, they were interested in the information, but they weren't interested in spending money. They were passive gawkers, not dedicated buyers. To add insult to injury, upon further research, Melissa found that other health experts and raw food specialists were monetizing their content. So why did it not work for her?

Melissa knew it was time to go back to the drawing board. Her business owner friends told her that she needed to start over and get in front of people who valued her expertise and were willing to pay for it. As long as she was giving away so many freebies and making herself so accessible, she would continue to attract the brain pickers. She reworked her marketing strategy, started purging her social media following and mailing list, and pulled back on the amount of information she shared freely. She decided to keep most of the links and access to the existing information available, but made sure to include information on how to move to the next step and work with her as a client. She also only made newer content available only to paying clients.

At first she got some push back and people were angry with her for changing up the rules of the game. But she didn't care. She had been spending way too much time on work that wasn't producing income, and if people didn't understand she had a business to run, well too bad for them. She could no longer dedicate her time to helping people who were only out for freebies.

After she implemented her new strategy, as always, there were a few people who continued to email her asking questions. Previously, she would give free consultations and advice to people when they needed advice, but it rarely lead to a conversion. Now, when she receives an email or an inquiry, she started asking qualifying questions to make sure the person wasn't just fishing for information. Some took exception to it, others played coy as if they were seriously looking for her help, but really wanted to pick her brain. She got more comfortable as time went on setting boundaries and not wasting her time on dead end prospect.

Melissa learned quickly how to qualify a potential client and when to direct people to her free content so she wouldn't waste her time. This reduced her stress and left more time for her to work with real clients and to continue building her brand. Whenever she encountered a habitual brain picker, she made it a point to politely refer them to Google. This experience taught her that she needed to be confident in her value and not let people assign it for her. Where as before she felt it was her obligation to get all people on a healthy life track, she now realized she was only obligated to her paying clients. Any guilt she felt or pressure to be seen as an authority went away as her sales increased.

Chapter 9

You're An Expert, Stand Your Ground

Most people are afraid to draw the hard lines in the sand for fear of angering a friend or losing a potential client or opportunity. Trust me, if they will walk away because they cannot get a freebie, they weren't meant to be a client and there was no real opportunity in it for you. Many in the marketing circles will tell you the free give away is vital. But it doesn't always lead to a sale. Likewise, giving away what you would do in a given situation during an interview will not necessarily lead to you being hired. It's up to you to determine what you're willing to give away, how much of it and to whom.

Don't back down. I know it's hard to say "no" sometimes. But you can't back down. People will know how far they can bend or push you. Stand firm, set your boundaries and guard your treasures (your brain and the know how in it). The minute you compromise, you devalue yourself and your expertise.

I spent a lot of years trying to compete with the big boys and wanting to be accepted. It was a compulsion that lead me to rack up many consultative hours with no pay. I trained people to think of me as a friend and not a professional. I was that go to lady that had all the answers. People assumed that because I didn't put myself up on a pedestal and that I remained approachable regardless of the number of speaking engagements or media interviews I had done, that they had a right to my help.

Some people don't know how to respect boundaries, but ultimately it's your responsibility to put them in place. Human beings by nature are going to try to get what they can with the least expense and least hassle for themselves. It's often not about the other person. And when you position yourself as that helpful, open and knowledgeable person, you become fair game.

I can argue all day long that it isn't fair and that people should respect me and what I bring to the table. But if I haven't been clear on boundaries or commanded respect, I can't complain but so much. At some point I needed to look inside myself, do a gut check, and reposition myself so that people took me seriously. You never see anyone pulling half the stuff they do on you on people like Oprah Winfrey, Martha Stewart, Warren Buffet, Bill Gates, Pete Cashmore, Sheryl Sandberg, Suze Orman, and countless others. They've established clear boundaries.

Oprah for instance is the queen of the giveaways. In 25 years, her brand was built on educating people and giving away free advice sixty minutes a day, five days a week. And as her brand grew, she started giving away material things and plugging products for authors, celebrities and even politicians. But nobody could just walk up to Oprah and say *hey, I have this problem, can you help me out*? You can't just walk up to her and ask her to give you a job or help you grow your business.

Suze Orman is America's financial expert. She spends an hour per week on television giving away all kinds of advice on finances, she counsels people on the spot (on her show) and she does speaking engagements. But try going up to Suze and asking her to help you get out of debt and she will direct you to any one of her products or services. She has limits and boundaries. Could some people get by on just the advice she gives out on television? Absolutely. But we all know that what she shares is generic in nature and each person's circumstances are different. To get to the meat of her advice, you have to buy her products or work with her, and that ain't free.

Just because you're not on television or radio, doesn't mean you are any less influential or deserving of respect. And just because you may only have two years into your career, doesn't make you any less knowledgeable than the person who has twenty years. They've just worked with more people than you have. No matter where you are in your career or business, you are still a professional. Don't let other people assign your value. I did it for far too long and excused it as paying dues. There is paying dues and there is getting taken. I've done both.

When my first business was starting out, I didn't have all the bells and whistles like today. It was the early 90's and the infancy stages of the Internet. So I couldn't compete with the big boys. Add to that, I was still learning my way around the recruiting industry. I had no mentors. I had a few clients. But the big companies that I did manage to land took advantage of me by getting "trial" service, demanding lower rates, and basically saying I wasn't in the big leagues yet so I had to accept whatever scraps came my way. For a long time, I believed that. It wasn't until I started training my brain to believe in my abilities and standing up for myself that things changed.

Fast forward to now, although I do know my value and I have set boundaries, I still find myself over sharing and being a brain picker magnet at times. When I made the conscious decision to engage in social media, start a show and write, I opened myself up to brain picking. I don't regret it because the person I am today is a far cry from the push over I was before. I've learned how to enforce limits. I know that doing all that I do, I foster an environment where people assume it's free to work with me.

But much like Oprah, Suze and others, I can give away the general free stuff. But I've positioned my business and my brand to be professional and can pick and choose who I want to *work with* and who I want to *give to*. I'm no longer in a place where I have to be in the public eye to build my street cred. I've done it already. I have nothing left to prove. I know what I bring to the table and I make no apologies.

I've confidently priced my products and services and those who truly want it, find a way to get it and pay for it. I no longer feel guilty for telling people *no* and it is so liberating. I don't beat myself up for deciding not to help someone any further than the free stuff. My conscience is clear. It is not my responsibility to save the world. It is my responsibility to grow my business, provide a future for my family and give my paying clients the best service and results they can expect of me. I will never apologize for that.

Know your worth and understand your value. Stop being taken advantage of. When you start clearly defining your boundaries, people will learn to respect them. Take pride in your work, be honest and people will respect you. As I've said several times in this book already, people will treat you the way you train them to treat you. You can't control people, but you can manage their expectations of you. Stand by your word, demand respect, and be confident in yourself. It's OK to give away some things some times, but don't ever put yourself out trying to win business that clearly isn't meant for you. Never be afraid to walk away and say *no more freebies*. Don't let people pick your brain because it does cost to maintain it.

My Story

This book wouldn't be complete if I didn't share the story behind the blog post, and ultimately, this book. I hope my story doesn't offend (if so, oh well), but serves to drive the point home as clearly as possible.

People say karma has a funny way of getting you when you least expect it. Good karma comes when you do good for others and put your needs secondary. Bad karma comes when you selfishly ignore the plight of others. But nobody ever talks about that middle ground. It's always either good or bad karma.

I was raised to be selfless and always think about other people before myself. Never ask people for anything, but always be willing to give freely whenever they needed me. My Dad exemplified this. He would give his last to help a person out and never ask for anything in return. Even when he knew the person's promises to pay him back were empty, he still gave.

I had seen him go above and beyond for family members, including one of my uncles, to make sure they were taken care of. They never bothered to pay him back, see if he needed anything, or when on the rare occasions he did need something, they claimed they didn't have it. But it never jaded him or stopped him from helping until the day he died.

I guess in a way, I carry that example around with me from my childhood. I always want my family and friends to do as well as or even better than I am, and I'm often puzzled when I want it for them more than they want it for themselves. Whenever I would learn about investing or entrepreneurship and try to share my new found knowledge with some of them, they'd say things like *why don't you learn it for both of us and just give me the cliff notes.* Or *you're so much better at this than I am. You do it and I'll just copy what you do.* It frustrated me to no end. But still, I continued to do and give, and rarely received in return.

As I got into my business and found my groove, I wanted as many of you do, to be a respected authority that people would feel comfortable turning to. The Internet allowed me to make that happen faster than any other methods I had tried before. Yes, I networked, and I believe I have grown a great circle of people that I can learn from and count on. But I wanted to follow my own rule of not limiting myself. There's a whole world of people out there and I wanted to get to know as many as I could.

When social media started catching on (not at all like it is today), I knew I had to be part of that movement. I had so much knowledge to share and I felt people could benefit from my expertise. If for nothing else, they could learn from some of my mistakes and avoid some of the obstacles I had encountered. So I began by blogging. It seemed harmless enough and I was able to express myself while still educating people. People slowly started finding my blog and sharing it with others. I knew I was on to something when the media started contacting me for sound bites or feature articles.

With the new-found attention, I felt like I wasn't attracting enough people, the right people. Sure people read my content, but other than a co-sign or an amen, people weren't moved to work with me. When blogging wasn't enough, I decided to up the ante and start writing more. I was able to write for some great websites and magazines, as you know, and my audience increased. It was phenomenal. People really loved my no nonsense approach and looked forward to my pieces. But still, all I managed to get were a few comments to my writing. Sure, they wrote and engaged in conversations to discuss my writing and opinions. But once again, I found myself in the same rut.

When I decided to do my radio show, it was a huge step for me. Now, my audience would get to hear me live, uncensored and unedited. I had no idea how they would react to it. I had no idea what I would say on the show. So after praying on it, I just went for it. At first I'd gotten a couple of listeners who found the show and listened. They would comment and send me email asking for additional information about whatever the topic was. I'd answer them, give advice, then move on to the next show.

Then the show started getting more popular. I had found my rhythm and started booking great guests. The show turned into a place where people could tune in to get their problems solved in 60 minutes. I felt that people didn't want the same old boring shows where the host pushed the guests new books, events, products, etc. I wanted it to be informative and a safe environment for people to ask questions. They loved it, I loved it. It was a hit. Then I started noticing that people were hungry for even more. They wanted more than what I was giving them on the show. They figured that if I was so willing to take calls, email, and comments live on the show, then I shouldn't mind getting an impromptu email or phone call.

I should have known better, but I decided to keep the momentum going on social media. As my Twitter count grew, I was engaging in more chats, answering questions, providing motivational and uplifting advice. I was a regular Dear Abby on

Twitter. The same thing happened on Facebook and in the Linked In forums. I had created a cycle that was moving so fast and furious, I was finding it harder to keep up and my sales were down. I could not understand it. I did everything I was supposed to do. I had the numbers (organically) and I didn't resort to trickery, spamming or funneling to grow my numbers. I gave my audience what they wanted...me. Uncensored, unedited me.

I found myself getting burned out. I had always vowed that I would never ignore anyone or pull an Oprah (sorry Oprah!!!) where I would just selectively respond or use my staff to push messages on my behalf. That was inauthentic and went against the premise of *social* media. I had a decision to make. Did I want to run a business or be popular? Did I want to save the world or save myself from losing it all?

My breaking point came long before I decided to write this wonderful article on Forbes. I had been so tired of people taking advantage of my kindness and abusing my trust. Yes, *abusing* is exactly the word I wanted to use. I had given so much and helped so many, and when I turned to some of the very people I helped, I was met with silence or shut doors. Now you'll probably throw my own words back at me and say *well they weren't your people anyway*. And you're right. They weren't. And I knew this going in. I'm a keen judge of character and I can smell a bullshitter a mile away. But, because of this karma thing, I still felt the need to help anyway. I figured as long as my conscience was clean who cared about their intentions.

Here's the problem with that thinking. It doesn't pay the bills. I found myself paying more attention to what other people wanted and less on what I needed. I created a variety of

132

programs, courses, books and services that would fit the masses. I got cheers and well wishes from a lot of the people I helped along with the empty gesture I'm sure you all have heard: *if you ever need anything, just let me know. I'm so proud of you and will support you in any way I can.* Uh huh. Any way except in dollars. Many of the people who had my back when I was dropping free knowledge, never even bothered to so much as buy a book. And when some of them did, it was *after* it was discounted to go on sale. What I learned from that experience is that I cannot rely on people in general, especially some people I know. I have gotten more business from strangers over the years than many of the people I had helped out gratis.

I have spent countless hours in coffee, breakfast and lunch meetings listening to and helping people out. There have been days where I was down to my last on gas and still drove to give courtesy consultations. I have driven in 100+ degree heat with no air conditioner in my car just to help someone figure out how to save their business. I have granted complimentary 30-minute consultations that dragged on for two hours. I've done the free speaking engagements where I wowed the audience, took questions and stayed until the very last person was helped- and not be allowed to sell or promote my business. I once drove 20 miles back to a restaurant to meet a woman who drove up from another county while I was in her town just so she wouldn't have a wasted trip...while I knew I had to be back to my hotel to get sleep so I could catch a 4AM flight back home.

I have done all of this and more for free, and I may have silently complained, but I never let anyone down. I've paid my dues and I've paid it forward 10,000 fold. So I feel I am qualified to say **enough**. Give a sister a break!

Do I regret it? Sometimes, yes I do. But again, it's my fault and I take full blame. I trained them on what to expect from me. Free advertisement, complimentary coaching, free books, an hour of my time here, unpaid speaking engagement there. It all adds up. I use to get so mad at people who would tell me to stop being nice to people. I felt they didn't understand. My karma account would balance out in the end. But as that weight caved in on me to always be on while still trying to produce revenue for my business, I cracked. I'm not ashamed to admit it. It had almost done me in and on a few occasions, I considered shutting down my business entirely and ending the brand. The brand had become synonymous with freebies.

So what do I gain from sharing this with you? Well first of all, I've come a long way, baby. I no longer feel the need to give all the time. I still gift to people and I keep my philanthropic work under wraps. It's nobody's business but mine, God and the person I'm gifting. I point people to all of my free resources and keep it moving. I now prequalify before I accept a phone call, meeting or invitation. I am very clear that I am a businesswoman first. It seems kind of harsh to some, but I like having a roof over my head and a bed to sleep in at night. I can't have that if I'm giving it all away all the time. I'm at a place of peace now. But it took a long time to get here. I still get brain pickers who try, and sometimes it is hilarious. But instead of anger, I feel pity for them because they don't know what they could get if they just took the time to value themselves by investing in the results, not the quick fixes.

I wrote this book because until I wrote that article, I had no idea how many people struggled with this as I had. Everyone has their own reasons and stories of how they ended up here. But we're all capable of turning it around. It is my hope that this book gives a voice to the shy, confidence to the weak and reinforcement to the forgetful. Sharing is great, but only when it is mutually beneficial. It is your responsibility to retrain people to give back even when they don't have the money to do it. Remind them there are other ways to reciprocate. I'll admit this isn't always easy to do. But I had to learn how to do it. I no longer let myself get short-changed. I have boundaries and I'm not afraid to tell people that and expect them to respect it. I will still continue to give, but it will be on my terms.

Here's my message to you habitual brain pickers. One day you're going to find yourself on the other side of the table. When you're excited about your brand new business or new found knowledge and want to make a living, remember how it was when you did the picking. I guarantee you the tables will turn and you will find yourself being asked for favors, giving away services and products and expected to always do for others while your bank account is steadily depleted. When that happens, think back to all the times you picked people's brains and thought you were getting over on them. Trust me, it won't feel very nice. Do unto others as you would have them do unto you. It's OK to get some things free. But think about what it does (or can do) to the person you're asking. When you make brain picking your life's work, karma will eventually come back to bite you in the ass.

About the Author

If you really want to know about me and my story, I suggest you check out my website bio. It's a lot more down to earth and gives you a better view of me as a total person. You can visit: **www.empowerme.org/index.php/about/our-ceo/**. I always include the "standard corporate" bio for my readers as well. So here you go:

Adrienne Graham is a serial entrepreneur and the CEO of TWO companies.

She is the CEO & Founder of **Empower Me! Corporation**, a media, publishing and education company for the career professional, entrepreneur and small business owner looking to grow. She is the voice behind *Views From the Top Radio Show* and the creative visionary responsible for *Empower Me! Radio, Empower Me Institute, Empower Me! Magazine, Empowered Woman TV, Next Level Business Strategies,* and *the Empower Me Network*. She has taken what started as a small professional network for women, and turned into an international power brand for men and women serious about professional and entrepreneurial growth.

Graham is a 19-year recruiting veteran and CEO of **Hues Consulting & Management, Inc**, a diversity recruitment consulting firm. The firm specializes in inclusive diversity recruiting, executive search, recruiter training and coaching, employment branding, recruitment process outsourcing, ATS implementation and strategy consulting for venture capital funded portfolio companies. She is a Certified Diversity

Recruiter, trainer and professional career consultant who has been tapped by major publications as a Subject Matter Expert in the areas of recruiting, career management, diversity and social media. She also conducts Career Strategy Programs for individuals who are serious about taking their careers to the next level.

She is known as a Networking Power Broker who has mastered traditional and social networking. As evidence, her smartphone contains some pretty powerful people she can turn to at any time for advice or just to chat. The author of three self-published books, she wrote THE BOOK on Fearless Networking and set the bar for how to network in the 21st century.

She has been featured in numerous publications and blogs, as well as TV and radio shows as a subject matter expert for recruiting, diversity, networking, social media, entrepreneurship, career management and small business. She has been featured in/on MSNBC, Black Enterprise, Inc Magazine, Financial Times, Essence Magazine, Entrepreneur Magazine to name a few. She has spoken on a panel for Women in Tech-Social Media at the UVA Darden School of Business, a small business tech panel for Black Enterprise Magazine's 2010 Entrepreneurs Conference, a panel on social media monitoring at the Atlanta Tribune's Moving Your Business Forward Conference and a panel on the importance of online communities at Social Biz Atlanta.

In 2010 her radio show was elected as a Top 100 Heavy Hitter Radio Show for Small Business (one of only 8 shows from BlogTalkRadio) by Small Business Trends and Empower Me! Corporation was selected as a Top 10 Savviest in Social Media by StartUp Nation. She has also appeared on Jansing & Company as a Jobs Expert on MSNBC. Her tweets have been quoted on MSNBC.com, Success Magazine and the Dylan Ratigan Show (MSNBC).

You can find her causing a ruckus on Forbes.com and making people think.

Seen in:

Resources

Empower Me! Corporation- http://www.empowerme.org

Empower Me! Institute- http://www.empowermeinstitute.com

Empower Me! Magazine-
http://www.empowermemagazine.com

Empower Me! Radio- http://www.empowermeradio.com

Views From the Top Radio Show-
http://www.blogtalkradio.com/viewsfromthetop

Next Level Business Growth Strategies Program-
http://www.nextlevelbizcoaching.com

Interview with Adrienne Graham- No You Can't Pick My Brain-
Women of Google+- January 2012-
http://www.youtube.com/watch?v=NixDljr_ysQ

No, You Can't Pick My Brain Radio Interview/Discussion- Views
from the Top Radio Show- April 22, 2011-

http://www.blogtalkradio.com/viewsfromthetop/2011/04/22/no-
you-cant-pick-my-brain

No, You Can't Pick My Brain article- Forbes.com- March 2011-
http://www.forbes.com/sites/work-in-progress/2011/03/28/no-
you-cant-pick-my-brain-it-costs-too-much/

Contact the Author

Mailing Address:

P.O. Box 863, Alpharetta, Georgia 30009-0863, USA

Phone:

+1 866.810.2525

Email:

info@empowerme.org

Social Media:

Amazon Author Central- http://www.amazon.com/Adrienne-D.-Graham/e/B0066O0EF0/ref=ntt_athr_dp_pel_1

Twitter- http://www.twitter.com/talentdiva

Google+- https://plus.google.com/116632553979056982414

Linked In- http://www.linkedin.com/in/adriennegraham

Facebook- http://www.facebook.com/adrienne.graham

Viadeo- http://us.viadeo.com/en/profile/adrienne.graham

Skype- adrienne.graham

Cinch.fm- http://www.cinch.fm/adgraham

Vimeo- http://www.vimeo.com/empowermeorg

YouTube- http://www.youtube.com/empowermemagazine

LiveStream- http://www.livestream.com/empowerme

Ustream- http://www.ustream.tv/user/empowermeorg

Tout- http://www.tout.com/u/adgraham

iTunes- http://itunes.apple.com/podcast/views-from-the-top-blog-talk-radio/id325399679

RSS Feed- http://feeds.feedburner.com/EmpowerMeCorporation

Join our mailing list to keep up on the latest news, growth strategies tips, and announcements from Adrienne Graham and Empower Me! Corporation

http://eepurl.com/hIuzo

Buy other titles by Adrienne Graham:

http://www.empowerme.org/index.php/about/products/

Adrienne D. Graham

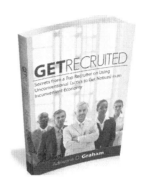

36430941R00095

Made in the USA
Lexington, KY
19 October 2014